101

solution-focused questions
for help with anxiety

THE 101 SOLUTION-FOCUSED QUESTIONS
SERIES OF BOOKS BY
FREDRIKE BANNINK

101 Solution-Focused Questions for Help with Anxiety

101 Solution-Focused Questions for Help with Depression

101 Solution-Focused Questions for Help with Trauma

Books available
separately or as a set.

A NORTON PROFESSIONAL BOOK

101

solution-focused questions for help with anxiety

FREDRIKE BANNINK

W.W. Norton & Company

New York | London

For information about permission to reproduce selections from this book,
write to Permissions, W. W. Norton & Company, Inc.,
500 Fifth Avenue, New York, NY 10110

For information about special discounts for bulk purchases, please contact W. W. Norton Special
Sales at specialsales@wwnorton.com or 800-233-4830

Manufacturing by RR Donnelley Westford
Book design by Molly Heron
Production manager: Christine Critelli

Library of Congress Cataloging-in-Publication Data

Bannink, Fredrike.
101 solution-focused questions for help with anxiety / Fredrike
Bannink.—First edition.
pages cm.—(A Norton professional book)
Includes bibliographical references and index.
ISBN 978-0-393-71108-0 (pbk.)
1. Anxiety—Treatment—Miscellanea. 2. Solution-focused brief therapy.
I. Title. II. Title: One hundred one solution-focused questions for help with anxiety.
III. Title: One hundred and one solution-focused questionsfor help with anxiety.
RC531.B26 2015
616.85'2206—dc23
                                    2015024255

W. W. Norton & Company, Inc.
500 Fifth Avenue, New York, N.Y. 10110
www.wwnorton.com

W. W. Norton & Company Ltd.
Castle House, 75/76 Wells Street, London W1T 3QT

1 2 3 4 5 6 7 8 9 0

"May your choices reflect
your hopes, not your fears."

———————

Nelson Mandela's quote
will be the theme
of this book.

Contents

Acknowledgments

According to Steve De Shazer, one of the founders of solution-focused brief therapy, differences in and of themselves are just differences. But some people (and some animals) have made a difference that has been significant in my life and my work. In one way or another, they all assisted me in writing these volumes.

I thank my friends, colleagues, students, and above all my clients, who have helped me discover, apply, and improve my work over the years. I also thank my publisher, Deborah Malmud, who kindly invited me to write this book series; my friend and translator, Suzanne Aldis Routh; and everyone else who has contributed to the realization of this book.

To my husband, I am grateful for your continuing love and support. To my four Italian cats, *mille grazie* for keeping me company during the many pleasant hours of writing.

101

solution-focused questions
for help with <u>anxiety</u>

Introduction

This is a book to help clients create a new and better life. It aims to help clients struggling with anxiety to enhance their well-being by being first and foremost a practical book for professionals working with clients suffering from anxiety, offering them solution-focused (SF) viewpoints and skills. The book invites all professionals (I will use the term *therapists*) to change their focus from what is wrong to what is right with clients and from what isn't working to what is working in their lives.

Traditional psychotherapy has been strongly influenced by the medical model.[1] The structure of problem-solving—first determining the nature of the problem and then intervening to minimize suffering—influences the content of the interaction between therapists and clients: The focus is

---

1 The medical model uses the term *patient*; solution-focused brief therapy uses the term *client*.

1

on pathology. However, it is not this negative way of thinking but clients' strengths, competencies, and resources that are most important in bringing about positive change. The secret of positive change is to focus all energy not on fighting the old, but on building the new.

This is Volume 1 of a series of three books, each offering 101 solution-focused questions to help with a specific psychiatric disorder: anxiety (this volume), depression (Volume 2), and trauma (Volume 3). The series—which may in the future include more titles—is based on my book *1001 Solution-Focused Questions: Handbook for Solution-Focused Interviewing* (Bannink, 2010a), originally written in Dutch and translated into English, German, and Korean.

I feel privileged that Insoo Kim Berg, co-founder of solution-focused brief therapy (SFBT), wrote the foreword of *1001 Solution-Focused Questions* in 2006, stating:

> SFBT is based on the respectful assumption that clients have the inner resources to construct highly individualized and uniquely effective solutions to their problems . . . The 1001 SF questions presented in this clear and well-written book will give the reader a very good idea of the importance of the precise use of language as a tool in SFBT. Readers are invited to open themselves to a new light on interviewing clients.

The focus in each volume is on creating preferred futures and the pathways to get there. In addition to a description of the way in which SFBT is applied, each book contains exactly 101 SF questions. Over the years, I have collected more than 2,000 SF questions. It has been quite a challenge to select what I think are the best 101 questions for each volume. I admit I cheated a little by sometimes grouping multiple questions together as one and by changing some questions to the first person (in this volume, only questions therapists ask their clients are counted). As a result, you actually get far more than 101 questions! Questions for therapists themselves and questions clients may ask themselves (sometimes invited by their therapists) or may ask their therapists are also described, but these are not included in the "101" list. At the end of each chapter, an overview of the SF questions is given. Some of the questions overlap with those in other chapters. Rather than repeating these questions, I have chosen to mention each SF question just once.

SFBT is a transdiagnostic approach. The reason I have nevertheless written separate volumes for different psychiatric disorders is to accommodate the many colleagues who are working with specific client groups. To give readers the opportunity to integrate the SF approach, this book introduces 29 exercises, 15 cases, and 16 stories.

This volume is aimed at all professionals working with clients suffering from anxiety, as well as family and friends, who would prefer to adopt a (more) positive approach and/or would like to simply increase the range of techniques available to them. SF conversations with clients have proven to be more lighthearted than other kinds of conversations, ensuring less burnout for therapists. Although the book is primarily aimed at therapists, I hope that people suffering from anxiety who don't see a therapist may also find useful information and helpful exercises contained within its pages.

It's about time to turn the tide on the treatment of anxiety and shift the focus from reducing distress and merely *surviving* to building success and positively *thriving*.

—Fredrike Bannink
December 2014

1

Anxiety

Introduction

The nature and function of fear and anxiety teach us much about the processes involved in abnormal anxiety. *Fear* is a present-oriented state that occurs in response to real or imagined danger. Some of these threats may be present in the here-and-now; others are a response to what is going on inside us (a disturbing physical sensation, a thought or memory) or a combination of these. Fear is characterized by an acute surge of the sympathetic branch of the autonomic nervous system, with intense physiological changes and action to fight or flee from signs of danger. There is a greater vigilance and a narrowing of attention so one stays focused on the event that elicits the fear (Barlow, 2002). Fear is highly adaptive because it serves an important function: to avert the threatening event.

Anxiety and *worry*, by contrast, are future-oriented mood states, accomplished by anxious apprehension, an increase in muscle tension, and EEG beta activity.

Anxiety is defined as "a state of intense apprehension, uncertainty, and fear resulting from the anticipation of a threatening event or situation, often to a degree that normal physical and psychological functioning is disrupted" (American Heritage Medical Dictionary, 2007, p. 38). Experiencing fear and anxiety is in many instances healthy and adaptive. Too much fear or anxiety, however, impedes one's ability to lead a normal life and take productive and effective action.

The focus in traditional psychotherapies is on reducing negative affect, whereas in solution-focused brief therapy (SFBT) the focus is on increasing positive affect to help clients make their lives better instead of bitter.

Anxiety

People who worry are typically anxious about something that may happen in the future, whereas people experiencing fear are afraid of what is happening right now.

Anxiety is marked by *what-if worries*. Physiological symptoms include muscle tension, heart palpitations, sweating, dizziness, and shortness of breath. Emotional symptoms include restlessness, a sense of impending doom, a fear of dying, a fear of embarrassment or humiliation, and a fear of something terrible happening. Cognitive models of anxiety emphasize an overdeveloped sensitivity to threat (Beck, Emery, & Greenberg, 1985). Behaviors most closely associated with anxiety are verbal or cognitive (e.g., worrying), whereas behaviors associated with fear involve actions such as escaping, fighting, or freezing. Severe anxiety is seen as a risk factor for suicide (Fawcett, 2013).

Anxiety disorders include panic attacks, panic disorder, agoraphobia, separation anxiety disorder, specific phobias, social phobia, generalized anxiety disorder, and selective mutism (voluntary refusal to speak). There is increasing empirical support for the notion that the self-defeating impact of *avoiding negative affect* is the core pathological process that fuels all anxiety disorders (Forsyth & Eifert, 1998). The chapter on anxiety disorder in the fifth edition of the *Diagnostic and Statistical Manual of Mental Disorders* (DSM-5; American Psychiatric Association, 2013) no longer includes obsessive-compulsive disorder (which is included with the obsessive-compulsive and related disorders) or stress disorder and acute stress disorder (which is included with the trauma- and stressor-related disorders). Close to 50% of individuals diagnosed with an anxiety disorder also meet the criteria for a depressive disorder (Batelaan et al., 2010; see Volume 2: Depression).

Although tending toward chronicity, anxiety disorders are responsive to psychotherapeutic *treatment* modalities. Shortly after completing their book on cognitive therapy for depression, Beck et al. (1985) developed a treatment manual for anxiety. A basic tenet was that the thinking present in anxiety is different from that present in depression: the *cognitive specificity hypothesis*. Depression was seen to be concerned with loss, whereas anxiety was seen to involve the perception of physical or psychosocial threat, together with an underestimate of coping and rescue factors.

Brewin (2006) states that vulnerability to emotional disorders lies in memory representations (e.g., negative self-schemas) that are activated by triggering events and maintain a negative mood. His research suggests that there are multiple memories involving the self that compete to be retrieved.

He suggests that CBT does not directly modify negative information in memory, but produces changes in the activation of positive and negative representations such that the positive ones are assisted to win the retrieval competition. His conclusion is that it may be unnecessary for negative thinking to be corrected; a person needs only to disengage from it.

Positive Emotions

In most psychotherapies, questions are asked about negative emotions, such as "How do you feel when you are having a panic attack?" or "How do you feel when you think people are watching you?" It is believed that getting clients to explore and express negative emotions is important in helping them. The traditional therapist's job is to minimize negative affect by dispensing drugs or instigating psychological interventions, thereby rendering people less anxious or depressed. The aim of traditional psychotherapy is to make miserable people less miserable. Therapists treat mental illness within the disease–patient framework of repairing damage; the focus is on pathology ("What's wrong with you?"). Therapists often forget to ask the question "What's right with you?"

The focus on pathology reflects the spirit of an age in which most disciplines focused on problems, and it also reflects the nature of emotions themselves. For example, the literature in psychology between 1970 and 2000 includes 46,000 papers about depression and 400 papers about joy (Myers, 2000). Overall, positive emotions are fewer in number than negative emotions. Generally speaking, there are three or four negative emotions for every positive emotion. Positive emotions are less differentiated than negative emotions, and this imbalance is also reflected in the number of words in most languages that describe emotions.

Recently, more attention has been paid to theories of positive emotions (interest, contentment, enjoyment, serenity, happiness, joy, pride, relief, affection, love). Positive affect offsets the deleterious physiological effects of stress through the neuroendocrine system. People who report finding positive meaning in response to a negative event have more adaptive hormonal responses, making them more resilient in the face of stressful events (Epel, McEwen, & Ickovics, 1998). This finding is further reinforced by research showing that positive and negative affect are associated with different neural structures (Cacioppo & Gardner, 1999).

Positive affect facilitates a broad range of important social behaviors and thought processes. It leads to greater creativity, improved negotiation processes and outcomes, and more thorough, open-minded, flexible thinking. Positive affect also promotes generosity and social responsibility in interpersonal interactions (Isen, 2005). People who are feeling happy are more likely to do what they want to do, more likely to want to do what is socially responsible and helpful and what needs to be done, enjoy what they are doing more, are more motivated to accomplish their goals, are more open to information and think more clearly. One of the most distinctive cognitive effects observed is increased flexibility and creativity. This may be mediated by release of the neurotransmitter dopamine. The *dopamine hypothesis* arose from the observation, at behavioral and cognitive levels, that positive affect fosters cognitive flexibility and the ability to switch perspectives (together with the fact that dopamine in the anterior cingulate region of the brain enables flexible perspective-taking).

Isen and Reeve (2005) found that positive emotions foster intrinsic motivation, as reflected by choice of activity in a free-choice situation and by the amount of enjoyment rated during a novel and challenging task. Positive emotions also promote responsible behavior in a situation where uninteresting tasks need to be done. This has implications for the relationship between positive affect and aspects of self-regulation, such as self-control.

Ways to increase positive affect include:

- *Positive reappraisal*: cognitive strategies for reframing a situation to see it in a more positive light (seeing the glass half full as opposed to half empty).
- *Coping*: efforts directed at solving or managing the problem that is causing distress.
- Infusion of ordinary events with *positive meaning*. People may be more likely to bring about, note, or remember positive events during chronically stressful conditions as a way of offsetting the negative affective consequences of a negative event.

The *broaden-and-build theory of positive emotions* (Fredrickson, 2003, 2009) suggests that positive emotions broaden one's awareness and encourage novel, varied, and exploratory thoughts and actions. Over time, this broadened behavioral repertoire builds skills and resources. This is in contrast with negative emotions, which promote narrow, immediate survival-oriented behavior. Fredrickson states that it is this narrowing effect on our thought–action repertories that distinguishes negative and positive affect. Negative emotions entrain people toward narrowed lines of thinking consistent with the specific action tendencies they trigger. Positive emotions broaden our thought–action repertoires and build enduring personal resources physically, intellectually, psychologically, and socially (for a description of the broaden-and-build-theory, see Volume 2: Depression).

EXERCISE 1. TURN POSITIVITY ON

We all have the power to turn positivity on and off. Experiment and turn positivity on. Whether you are sitting in your living room, using the bathroom, driving your car, or riding a bus or train, ask yourself, "What is right about my current circumstances?" "What makes me lucky to be here?" "What aspect of my current situation might I view as a gift to be treasured?" "How does it benefit me or others?" Taking time to think in this manner ignites gratitude. Take a few moments to savor and enjoy this good feeling.

Now turn positivity off. Examples of positivity-spoiling questions are "What is wrong here?" "What is bothering me?" "What should be different and better?" "Who is to blame?" Ask yourself these questions, follow the chain of thoughts they produce, and see how quickly positivity plummets (Fredrickson, 2009).

Contrary to traditional psychotherapies, SFBT aims to increase *positive emotions*. "How will you feel when your best hopes are met?" "What will you be thinking, doing, and feeling differently when you notice that the steps you are taking are in the right direction?" Bringing back the best from the past by asking questions about previous successes and competence also triggers positive emotions. Asking solution-focused (SF) questions such as "How will you know this session has been useful?" serves to widen the array of thoughts and actions available to clients. Using imagination, as in the *miracle question* or other future-oriented techniques (see Chapter 5), also creates positive emotions and has a powerful impact on clients' capacity to expand ideas and activities. The use of compliments and competence questions such as "How did you manage to do that?" further elicits positive emotions. SF therapists notice their clients' competence and resources and compliment them or play those resources back to them (see Chapter 6). SFBT helps to create an atmosphere in which positive emotions flourish and the problem can be transformed into something positive: a new and better life.

Grant and O'Connor (2010) found that reducing negative emotions doesn't automatically increase positive emotions. They noticed different effects resulting from problem-focused and SF questions in a coaching context. Problem-focused questions (e.g., "What is bothering you?") reduce negative affect and increase self-efficacy, but they don't increase positive affect or one's understanding of the nature of the problem. SF questions also reduce negative affect and increase self-efficacy, but in addition they increase positive affect and one's understanding of the nature of the problem.

STORY 1. THE NUN STUDY

"And they lived happily ever after." Autobiographies from 180 Catholic nuns, composed when they were a mean age of 22 years, were scored for emotional content and then related to their survival rates between the ages of 75 to 95. A strong inverse association was found between positive emotional content in these writings and mortality. As the quartile ranking of positive emotion in early life increased, there was a likewise decrease in risk of mortality, resulting in a 2.5-fold difference between the lowest and highest quartiles. Positive emotional content in early-life autobiographies was strongly associated with longevity six decades later (Danner, Snowdon, & Friesen, 2001).

Balancing Positive and Negative Emotions

Negative emotions are as much a part of the richness of life as positive emotions. They serve as important a function as does physical pain, alerting us to problems that may need to be addressed. Therefore, negative emotions should be appreciated as a natural and even useful aspect of our everyday lives.

Fredrickson's *positivity ratio*—comparing positive and negative thoughts, emotions, and activities—shows a tipping point around the 3 (positive) to 1 (negative) mark. At this place, people experience transformed lives through positivity. For those with ratios exceeding 3 to 1, positivity forecasts both openness and growth. Below this ratio, people may get pulled into a downward spiral fueled by negativity and may become depressed. Above this 3 to 1 ratio, people are drawn along an upward spiral energized by positivity (Fredrickson, 2009).

Well-being is a function of three factors: high positive affect, low negative affect, and high life satisfaction. A key to flourishing is having a high positive-to-negative emotion ratio. The good news is that we can improve our state by increasing positive emotions or decreasing negative ones (or both). For individuals, marriages (Gottman, 1994), and business teams, flourishing—that is, doing remarkably well—comes with positivity ratios above 3 to 1. By contrast, people who don't overcome depression, couples who fail in their marriages, and business teams that are unpopular and unprofitable have ratios even below 1 to 1. Although there has been some criticism about the empirical evidence of the positivity ratio, the fact that positivity is important in people's lives remains untouched.

STORY 2. THE DOG I FEED MOST

A Native American elder described his inner struggle in this manner: "Inside of me there are two dogs. One is mean and evil; the other dog is good. The mean dog fights the good dog all the time." When his grandson asked him which dog won, the elder replied, "The one I feed most."

We want to feel pleasure and avoid pain, and although people generally prefer happiness, they often prefer being angry or anxious, as they see this emotion as providing more benefits. Tamir, Mitchell, and Gross (2008) tested whether people prefer to experience emotions that are potentially useful, such as anger or fear, even when they are unpleasant. They tested whether individuals are motivated to increase their level of anger when they expect to complete a task where anger might enhance performance. Participants were told that they would play either a violent or a nonviolent computer game. They were asked to rate the extent to which they wanted like to engage in different activities before playing the game. Participants preferred activities that were likely to make them angry (e.g., listening to anger-inducing music, recalling past events in which they were angry) when they expected to play a violent game. Participants preferred more pleasant activities when they expected to play a nonviolent game. To examine whether preferences to increase anger resulted in improved performance, participants were assigned at random to either an angry, neutral, or excited emotion induction and then played a violent and a nonviolent computer game. As expected, angry participants performed better in the violent game, by killing more "enemies." However, angry participants didn't perform better in the nonviolent game, which involved serving customers. A factor that ought to be considered, where anger is concerned, is that it can be arousing, and can actually feel good in a certain way.

Interestingly, people sometimes opt for less pleasant feelings such as fear. This is particularly true when people are pursuing avoidance goals rather than approach goals. *Approach goals* seek out a positive outcome, as in "I will go to bed early tonight because I want to feel fit tomorrow morning." *Avoidance goals* seek to avoid a negative outcome, as in "I don't want to go to bed late tonight, because I don't want to be sleepy at work tomorrow morning." Tamir et al. (2008) found that people may prefer fear when they are pursuing avoidance goals. Despite the unpleasantness of fear, people recognize that it helps them to better achieve certain types of goals.

SF questions in this chapter are:

1. "How will you feel when your best hopes are met?"
2. "What will you be thinking, doing, and feeling differently when you notice that the steps you are taking are in the right direction?"
3. "How will you know this session has been useful?"

In the next chapter, we will take a closer look at solution-focused brief therapy and the many SF questions that lie at the heart of SFBT.

2

Solution-Focused
Brief Therapy

Introduction

Solution-focused brief therapy (SFBT) assists clients in developing a vision of a better future and in directing both clients and therapists toward a deeper awareness of the strengths and resources that clients can use in turning vision into reality (De Jong & Berg, 2002, p. xiii). In this chapter, a description of SFBT is followed by a short description of its theory, history, indications, and research.

Solution-focused (SF) questions lie at the heart of SFBT: They invite clients to think differently, to notice positive differences, and to help make desired changes. Four basic SF questions are presented as well as the research on microanalysis of dialogue in psychotherapy.

Solution-Focused Brief Therapy

SFBT is the pragmatic application of a set of principles and tools, best described as finding the direct route to what works. If something works (better), do more of it; if something isn't working, do something else.

The nature of SFBT is nonacademic; the pursuit is finding what works for this client at this moment in this context. The emphasis is on constructing solutions as a counterweight to the traditional emphasis on the analysis of problems. SFBT does not claim to solve peoples' problems or to cure their disorders. However, it claims to help clients achieve their preferred future, so classification or diagnosis of problems is often irrelevant. Of course, when clients achieve their preferred future, their fears, worries and anxiety might . . . or might not . . . have gone away (Bannink & Jackson, 2011).

SFBT is a competence-based approach, which minimizes emphasis on past failings and problems and instead focuses on clients' strengths, previous successes, and exceptions (times when the problem could have happened but didn't). In solutions-building, clients are seen as experts with regard to their own lives. SF therapists listen for openings in conversations that are often problem-saturated. These openings can be about what clients would like to be different, exceptions, competencies and resources, and who or what might be helpful in taking next steps. The clients' solutions are not necessarily related to any identified problem. Clients are encouraged to find out what works and increase the frequency of useful behaviors. Improvement is often realized by redirecting attention from dissatisfaction about the status quo to a positive goal and to take steps in that direction. This process of shifting attention uses three steps:

1. Acknowledge the problem: "This must be difficult for you."
2. Suggest a desire for change: "So I guess you would like things to be different . . ."
3. Ask about the preferred future: "How would you like things to be different?"

SFBT is based on *social constructionism*. This theory claims that the individual's notion of what is real—including his or her sense of the nature of problems, abilities, and possible solutions—is constructed in daily life in communication with others. People confer meaning on events in communication with others, and in this process language plays a central role. Shifts in perceptions and definitions occur within frames of reference within society; conferring meaning is not an isolated activity. Individuals adjust the way in which they confer meaning under the influence of the society in which they live.

The social constructionist perspective can be used to examine how therapists and conversations with them contribute to the creation of a new reality for clients. Clients' capacity for change is related to their ability to see things differently. These shifts in perception and the definition of reality occur in the SF conversation about the preferred future and exceptions. SF questions map out the clients' goal and solutions, which are assumed to be present in their life already.

De Shazer, Berg, and their colleagues developed SFBT during the 1980s. They expanded upon the findings of Watzlawick, Weakland, and Fisch (1974), who found that the attempted solution often perpetuates the problem and that an understanding of the origins of the problem is not (always) necessary. De Shazer's (1985) propositions include the following:

- The development of a solution is not necessarily related to the problem. Analysis of the problem isn't useful in finding solutions, whereas analysis of exceptions to the problem is.
- Clients are the experts. They determine the goal and the road to achieving this;
- If it isn't broken, don't fix it. Leave alone what is positive in the perception of clients.
- If something works, continue with it, even though it may be something different from what was expected.
- If something doesn't work, do something else. More of the same leads nowhere.

De Shazer and his colleagues discovered that three types of therapist behavior made clients four times as likely to talk about solutions, change, and resources:

1. *Eliciting questions*: "What would you like to see instead of the problem?"
2. *Questions about details*: "What exactly did you do differently?"

3. *Verbal rewards* (giving compliments) and *competence questions*: "How did you manage to come here today?"

SFBT is *indicated* for all work environments as a monotherapy or in combination with a problem-focused therapy. Depending on the nature of the problem, a problem-focused approach may be chosen (e.g., pharmacotherapy), in which the supplementary use of SFBT is often valuable. The attitude of the therapist, attention to goal formulation, and tapping into the often surprisingly large arsenal of competencies possessed by the client and his or her environment are key elements in a successful outcome. SFBT is also suitable for treating addiction-related problems, due to the considerable attention paid to the client's motivation to change.

Can SFBT be applied in cases of chronic and severe mental illness? The answer is that in these cases also, there are always people who can, as much as possible, beyond and outside the mental illness, reclaim their life and identity. O'Hanlon and Rowan (2003, p. ix) state,

> Over time, we have become increasingly convinced that traditional pathological language, labels, belief systems, and treatment methods can inhibit positive change. In fact, a hopeless situation can be engendered with unintentional and unfortunate cues from treatment milieus, therapists, family members, and oneself. Iatrogenic discouragement—that which is inadvertently induced by treatment—is often the result of such an unfortunate view of human perception and behavior.

STORY 3. SHOT BY A POISONED ARROW

If a man is shot by a poisoned arrow and says, "Don't take this arrow away before you find out exactly by whom and from where and how it was shot," the man's death is inevitable.

—BUDDHA

SFBT requires no extensive *diagnosis*. "Interventions can initiate change without the therapist's first understanding, in any detail, what has been going on" (De Shazer, 1985, p. 119). One may choose to commence treatment immediately and if necessary pay attention to diagnostics at a later stage. Severe psychiatric disorders or a suspicion thereof justifies the decision to conduct a thorough diagnosis, since the tracing of the underlying organic pathology, for instance, has direct therapeutic consequences.

During the first or follow-up sessions, it will automatically become clear whether an advanced diagnosis is necessary—for example, if there is a deterioration in the client's condition or if the treatment fails to give positive results. One could think of *stepped diagnosis* as being analogous to *stepped care* (Bakker, Bannink, & Macdonald, 2010).

Duncan (2010) states that, unlike with medical treatments, diagnosis is an ill-advised starting point for psychotherapy. Diagnosis in mental health is not correlated with outcome or length of stay, and giving the *dodo verdict* (all psychotherapies are equal and have won prizes) cannot provide reliable guidance regarding the best approach to solving a problem. Furthermore, a diagnosis should not be a label, but should lead to a kind of support that allows clients to reach their full potential.

Is it possible to solve problems without even talking about them? The answer is yes. Just say, "Suppose there is a solution" and invite clients to think about:

- What difference that solution will make in their lives and that of important others
- What they will be doing (and/or thinking and feeling) differently
- Who will be the first to notice
- What will be the first small sign that a solution is under way
- Who will be the least surprised
- What else will be better

Nowadays, the SF approach is being successfully applied to psychotherapy, coaching, conflict management and mediation, leadership and management, education and supervision, and sports. SFBT is based on over 20 years of theoretical development, clinical practice, and empirical *research*. Franklin, Trepper, Gingerich, and McCollum (2012) state that SFBT is an evidence-based form of psychotherapy. Meta-analytic reviews of the outcome research show SFBT to have a small to moderate positive outcome for a broad range of topics and populations. When SFBT has been compared with established treatments in recent, well-designed studies, it has been shown to be equivalent to other evidence-based approaches, producing results in substantially less time and at less cost. Gingerich and Peterson (2013) reviewed 43 studies. Thirty-two (74%) studies reported significant positive benefit from SFBT; 10 (23%) reported positive trends. These studies provide evidence that SFBT is an effective treatment for a wide variety of behavioral and psychological outcomes and, in addition, is briefer and therefore less costly than traditional approaches.

Problem-Talk or Solutions-Talk

SF therapists use operant conditioning principles during sessions. Operant conditioning deals with reinforcement and punishment to change behavior. They use the positive reinforcement of solutions-talk (paying attention to conversations about goals, exceptions, possibilities, competencies, and resources) and the negative punishment of problem-talk (withholding attention from conversations about problems, causes, impossibilities, and weaknesses). This doesn't mean that clients are not allowed to talk about problems or that SFBT is problem-phobic. Therapists listen respectfully to their client's story, but they don't seek any details about the presented problems, thus not reinforcing problem-talk (see Table 2.1).

TABLE 2.1

Differences between Problem-Talk and Solutions-Talk

Problem-Talk	Solutions-Talk
Conversations about problems, what clients don't want, causes, negative emotions, disadvantages, deficits, risks, failures, and the undesired/feared future	Conversations about what clients want, exceptions, positive emotions, advantages, strengths and resources, opportunities, successes, and the preferred future

EXERCISE 2. PROBLEM-TALK AND SOLUTIONS-TALK

Talk for five minutes with a colleague about a problem, worry, or annoyance he or she is experiencing. Ask your colleague problem-focused questions, such as "How long have you experienced this?" "How severe is it?" "How does it bother you?" "What else is troubling you?" "In what other areas of your life does this problem affect you?"

Talk again for five minutes about the same problem, worry, or annoyance, but now ask SF questions such as "What would you like to have instead of the problem?" "What have you tried to do that was helpful (even just a little bit)?" "When is the problem absent or less noticeable?" Or ask a question about the goal: "What would you like to have accomplished by the end of this session so that you can say it has been useful?" Together with the other person, note the differences between the two conversations. You may sense a lighter tone and a more optimistic mood when you talk about positive experiences, whereas a certain heaviness often accompanies problem-focused conversations. It is also possible that your colleague has already solved the problem or knows what to do to reach his or her goal.

Then reverse roles: Now you answer while the other person talks with you about your problem, worry, or annoyance. For the first five minutes, your colleague will use problem-focused questions; for the next five minutes, he or she will use SF questions. Together, again note the differences between the two conversations.

Solution-Focused Questions

The answers you get depend on the questions you ask. Solution-focused questions form a large part of the SF therapist's tool kit; they lie at the heart of SFBT. The questions invite clients to think about transformation and help them make desired changes in their life. Asking SF questions is not meant to gather information to become an expert on clients' lives. Rather, they are an invitation to think differently—to notice positive differences and make progress.

The attitude of SF therapists is one of *not knowing*. They allow themselves to be informed by their clients and the context of their clients' lives, which determines in what way solutions are devised. Another aspect of this attitude is *leading from one step behind*. In this, therapists, metaphorically speaking, stand behind their clients and tap them on the shoulder with SF questions, inviting them to look at their preferred future and, in order to achieve this, to envision a wide horizon of possibilities.

With SF questions, therapists ask clients to describe the smallest signs of progress and encourage them to carry on with the smallest and easiest of these. This enables clients to experience control over the problem in a safe and gradual manner, without becoming afraid or feeling overwhelmed by tasks for which they are not yet ready. These small changes pave the way for increasingly larger changes. SF questions are effective in encouraging clients to participate in and develop their own treatment plan, with which, implicitly, a context of hope is created (Dolan, 1991).

Communication is the tool of psychotherapy just as physical instruments are the tools of surgery, and we should treat therapeutic communication equally carefully and precisely. *Microanalysis of dialogue* (Bavelas, Coates, & Johnson, 2000) aims for a detailed and replicable examination of observable communication sequences between therapists and clients as they proceed in a dialogue, with an emphasis on the function of these sequences within the dialogue. Two tools are being observed when analyzing video recordings of the dialogues: analysis of *formulations* and analysis of *questions*. Formulations are a way for therapists to display their understanding of what clients have said:

- Clients present information ("I don't know what to do anymore")
- Therapists display their understanding with a formulation ("Do you mean you are at your wits' end?")
- Clients acknowledge, explicitly or implicitly, that the formulation is or is not a correct understanding ("Yes, that's right")

Another tool is the analysis of how *questions* function (intentionally or not) as therapeutic interventions. The impact of a question begins with its (often implicit) presuppositions, assumptions that form the background of the question. Questions from different therapeutic approaches demonstrate how the therapist's story shapes these presuppositions. In a problem-focused conversation, the question might be "Could you please tell me more about the problem you want to address today?"; whereas in an SF conversation, the question might be "What will be the best result of our session today?"

The content of each question or formulation can be positive, negative, or neutral.

Bavelas and colleagues (2000) use microanalysis to analyze expert sessions on SFBT and client-centered therapy (De Shazer and Berg for SFBT; Rogers and Raskin for CCT). Results show that the SF and client-centered experts differ in how they structure the sessions: Client-centered therapists use formulations almost exclusively, that is, they respond to client contributions. SF experts use both formulations and questions, that is, they both initiate and respond to client contributions. They also differ in the tenor of their contributions: SF therapists' questions and formulations are primarily positive, whereas those of client-centered therapists are primarily negative and rarely neutral or positive. *Positive therapist content* includes question, statements, formulations, or suggestions by therapists that focus clients on some positive aspect of their life (e.g., a relationship, trait, or experience in the past, present, or future). *Positive client content* includes questions, statements, formulations, or suggestions by clients that focus on some positive aspect of their life (e.g., a relationship, trait, or experience in the past, present, or future). Negative therapist or client content is the opposite.

When the therapist's utterance is positive, clients are more likely to say something positive, whereas when the therapist's utterance is negative, clients are more likely to say something negative.

Three SFBT and three CBT expert sessions (Meichenbaum was one of the CBT therapists) were also compared. The content of the SF therapists was significantly more positive and less negative than that of the CBT therapists. Across all therapists, clients' responding in positive talk led to more positive talk, and negative talk led to more negative talk. Thus, the therapists' use of positive content contributes to the co-construction of an overall positive session, whereas negative content does the reverse. The third finding was that, as a group, the SFBT experts were consistently more positive than negative, whereas the CBT experts differed widely among themselves (Franklin et al., 2012).

Microanalysis can complement outcome research by providing evidence about what therapists do and how the co-constructive nature of *language* is important in dialogues. Co-constructing a dialogue may be compared to a dance, or a duet, between therapists and clients. Some useful ideas for *paying attention to language* are:

- Change "if" to "when": "If I get over these panic attacks, I will be able to do what I want" becomes "When I get over these panic attacks, I will be able to do what I want."
- Change "can't" to "not yet": "I can't put the past behind me" becomes "I haven't yet been able to put the past behind me."
- Move problems from internal to external: "I am anxious" becomes "Anxiety has been visiting me for a while"; "I am a negative person" becomes "Negativity speaks to me regularly, and mostly I listen to what it says."
- Use the past tense when talking about problems, and the future tense when talking about what clients want to be different in their lives: "I will never get over this" becomes "So until now I haven't been able to get over what happened to me. How will my life be different when I am able to do that?"

EXERCISE 3. OPENING QUESTION

What *opening question* do you start a (first) session with? Do you opt for a problem-focused question ("What is the problem?" or "What is bothering you?")? Do you choose a neutral question ("What brings you here?")? Do you ask a question that implies you will work hard ("What can I do for you?")? Or do you ask an SF question ("What would you like to see different in your life?" or "When can we stop seeing each other?") or the *miracle question* (see Chapter 5)? Try out all possibilities and notice the differences in your clients' reactions.

Four Basic SF Questions

Four basic SF questions (Bannink, 2007, 2010a) can be used at the start of therapy or at the beginning of each session (e.g., "What are your best hopes for this session?"):

1. "What are your best hopes?"
2. "What difference will that make?"
3. "What works?"
4. "What will be the next signs of progress?" or "What will be your next step?"

The *first basic SF question* is: "What are your best hopes?"

Hope is one of the most powerful attitudes, emotions, thoughts, beliefs, and motivators. It is vital to human beings; it keeps people alive. It gets people out of bed in the morning. Hope keeps us going, even in the face of severe adversity. Hope whispers "Try it one more time" when the world says "Give up."

Offering a vision that change is possible and that there are better ways to deal with the situation is important in therapy. SFBT fits well with this value, because solutions-building is about the development of a well-defined goal through asking about client's best hopes and what differences those will make. These questions encourage clients to develop a detailed vision of what their lives might look like. It fosters hope and motivation and promotes self-determination. SFBT also counters any tendency to raise false hope in clients. Clients define their own visions for change and, as experts about their situation, clarify what parts of the preferred future can and cannot happen.

Questions about hope are different from questions about expectations. This may invite clients to look at the therapist for the solution of the problem.

The *second basic SF question* is: "What difference will that make?" Clients are invited to describe their preferred future in positive, concrete, realistic terms. How will they react, and how will they interact differently? How will their life be different? What will they be doing differently so that others will know that they have reached their preferred future? Often the preferred future is described without the problem that brought them to therapy, although some clients describe their preferred future with the problem still present, but without it bothering them so much anymore.

De Shazer (1991) states that it is *difference itself* that is an important tool for therapists and clients. In and of themselves, differences don't work spontaneously. Only when recognized can they be put to work to create a difference. Finding exceptions is another way of asking about differences. "When the problem is/was there to a lesser extent, what is/was different? What are/were you doing differently? What are/were other people doing differently?" Or "When is/was there a glimpse of the preferred future (the goal) already?" This reveals what was working in better times; some things that were helpful in the past may be used anew. Also, *scaling questions* help to find positive differences. Scaling questions can be asked about progress, hope, motivation, or confidence (see Chapter 6).

EXERCISE 4. SUPPOSE THINGS COULD CHANGE

Invite clients to think of something they would like to see changed. Ask, "Supposing things could change, what difference will that make? What else will be different? What else?" See how they will probably come up with more things than you or they imagined they would (this is called the *upward arrow technique,* as a counterweight to the downward arrow technique used in CBT, described in Bannink [2012a, 2014a]).

The third basic SF question is: "What works?"

Therapists may start by inquiring about *pretreatment change* (see Chapter 4). Most clients have tried other ideas before seeing a therapist. It is a common assumption that clients begin to change when therapists start to help them with the problem, but change is happening in all clients' lives. When asked, two thirds of clients in psychotherapy report positive change between the time they made the appointment and the first session (Weiner-Davis, de Shazer, & Gingerich, 1987). Exploration of pretreatment change often reveals new and useful information. When clients report that things are better, even just a little bit, ask competence questions: "How did you do that?" "How did you decide to do that?" "Where did you get this good idea?"

Exception-finding questions are frequently used to find out what works (see Chapter 6). These questions are new to many clients (and therapists), who are more accustomed to problem-focused questions. When asked about exceptions, which are the keys to solutions, they may start noticing them for the first time. Solutions are often built from formerly unrecognized positive differences. Therapists, having explored these exceptions, then compliment clients for all the things they have done.

A *scaling question* may be added: "On a scale where 10 equals you reached your preferred future and 0 equals the moment you picked up the phone to make this appointment, where would you say you are right now?" (see Chapter 6).

The *fourth basic SF question* is: "What will be the next signs of progress?" or "What will be your next step?" By asking "What will be *your* next step?"

therapists invites clients to—maybe for the first time—actually think about what they themselves can do to ameliorate the situation instead of waiting for other(s) or the therapist to provide a solution.

This question is only asked when clients want or need to go up further on the scale of progress. When the current state is the best possible state at that moment, then the conversation continues by asking clients how they can maintain the status quo. The question about the next signs of progress is open as to who should do what and when. A sign of progress may also be something that could happen without the clients taking action. Instead of focusing on the inner life of clients and why the problems arose, SF therapists invite clients to move into action.

The four basic SF questions can be seen as *skeleton keys*: keys that fit in many different locks. The locks (e.g., each problem) don't have to be explored and analyzed before these keys can be used. The keys can be used for all Axis I and Axis II psychiatric disorders.

CASE 1. WORKING FROM THE FUTURE BACK

SFBT works from the future back. The client suffering from a generalized anxiety disorder is invited to think about the following:

- "Suppose I made a full recovery. What would have helped me recover?"
- "How would I have found the courage to do that?"
- "What would have given me the strength to make these changes?"

- ■ "How would important people in my life (partner, friends, colleagues) tell that I had made a full recovery?"
- ■ "What, in their opinion, would have helped me to recover?"

SF questions in this chapter are:

4. "How would you like things to be different?" or "What would you like to see instead of the problem?"
5. "What exactly did you do differently?"
6. "How did you manage to come here today?"
7. "Suppose there is a solution . . . ?"
8. "What have you tried to do that was helpful (even just a little bit)?"
9. "When is the problem absent or less noticeable?"
10. "What would you like to have accomplished by the end of this session so that you can say it has been useful?" or "What will be the best result of our session today?"
11. "When can we stop seeing each other?"
12. "What are your best hopes? What difference will that make?"
13. "What works?"
14. "What will be the next signs of progress?" or "What will be your next step?"
15. "When the problem is/was there to a lesser extent, what is/was different then? What are/were you doing differently? What are/were other people

doing differently?" or "When is/was there a glimpse of your preferred future (the goal) already?"

16. "Supposing things could change, what difference will that make? What else will be different? What else?"

17. "On a scale where 10 equals you have reached your preferred future and 0 equals the moment you picked up the phone to make this appointment, where would you say you are right now?" (Plus all the follow-up scaling questions.)

In the next chapter, we will look at several traditional, as well as the SF, approaches to anxiety. An overview of the differences between these approaches is given. Traditional and SF approaches may also be combined in helping clients to reach their preferred future.

3

Therapeutic Approaches to Anxiety

Introduction

In this chapter, several traditional approaches to anxiety are described, as well as the solution-focused (SF) approach. Slowly but surely, a shift from a deficit focus to a resource focus in psychiatry and psychology has become noticeable. An overview of the differences between the two paradigms is given. Traditional and SF approaches may also be combined in helping clients to reach their preferred future.

Traditional Approaches to Anxiety

Most psychotherapeutic models apply the pathology model. Their aim is to reduce distress using the problem-solving paradigm. Among these models are psychoanalytic, client-centered, and cognitive behavioral therapy (CBT) approaches.

Cognitive models of anxiety emphasize an overdeveloped sensitivity to threat (Beck, Emery, & Greenberg, 1985). Clients suffering from anxiety need to better assess the risk of situations they fear. They also need to decrease their avoidance and confront situations they fear so they can test their negative predictions behaviorally. When clients learn to evaluate their thinking in a more realistic and adaptive way, they will experience improvement in their emotional state and behavior. CBT therapists also work at a deeper level of cognition: clients' core beliefs about themselves, their world, and other people. Modification of underlying dysfunctional beliefs may produce more enduring change.

Exposure therapy asks clients to confront or imagine a fearful situation. Exposure can be *in vivo* (real life), *in vitro* (imaginal), or *interoceptive*, where clients confront feared bodily symptoms such as an increased heart rate. With *systematic desensitization*, clients imagine situations they fear while the therapist helps them relax and cope with their fear reaction and eventually eliminate the anxiety. The imagery of the anxiety-producing situations gets progressively more intense until clients approach the anxiety-causing situation in real life (*graded exposure*). Exposure may be increased to the point of *flooding*, providing maximum exposure to the real situation. By repeatedly pairing a desired response (relaxation) with a fear-producing situation (e.g., open, public spaces) clients become desensitized to the old response of fear and learn to react with feelings of relaxation.

Lately there has been a noticeable shift in focus in CBT. For example, Beck (2011) emphasizes the positive, stating that most clients tend to focus unduly on the negative. Their difficulty in processing positive data leads them to develop a distorted sense of reality. To counteract this feature, therapists should help clients to attend to the positive. According to Beck, clients are invited to:

- Elicit their strengths ("What are some of my strengths and positive qualities?") at the evaluation of therapy [FB: In my opinion, this is a bit late]
- Find positive data from the preceding week ("What positive things happened since I came here last?")
- Seek data contrary to their negative automatic thoughts and beliefs ("What is the positive evidence that perhaps my thought isn't true?")
- Look for positive data ("What does this say about me?")
- Note instances of their positive coping

Furthermore, the therapeutic alliance should be used to demonstrate that therapists see clients as valuable human beings. Therapists can also suggest homework to facilitate their clients' experiencing pleasure and achievement.

Bannink (2012a, 2014a) developed a new form of CBT, which she calls *Positive CBT*. In this approach, SFBT, positive psychology, and traditional CBT are integrated. For example, in positive CBT, functional behavior analyses are made of exceptions to the problem instead of the problem itself. Monitoring is about exceptions, and the downward arrow technique, which focuses on beliefs that underpin negative reactions to a given situation, is replaced with the upward arrow technique, which focuses on beliefs that underpin positive reactions and exceptions to the problem.

The use of *imagery* in psychotherapy has a long history, and there is evidence of the significance of imagery in a number of psychological disorders. From the start, cognitive therapy emphasized the role of mental imagery. Contending that mental activity may take the form of words and phrases or images, affective distress can be directly linked to visual cognitions—as well as to verbal cognitions—and modifying upsetting visual cognitions can lead to significant cognitive and emotional shifts. Imagery plays an important role in CBT interventions like systematic desensitization and flooding (see earlier).

Imagery rescripting (ImRs) modifies a distressing image to change associated negative thoughts, feelings, and/or behaviors. Arntz and Weertman (1999) describe the use of ImRs to treat nightmares, posttraumatic stress disorder, bereavement, intrusive images, and eating disorders. ImRs is used not only to overcome problems, but also to help clients to develop a positive view of themselves and to promote self-determination and well-being.

Intrusive images are very common in psychological disorders and are therefore an obvious target for imagery-based interventions. Additionally, clients often experience an absence of positive, adaptive imagery. For example, happy, predictive images of the future are often lacking in depression and generalized anxiety disorder (Hackmann, Bennett-Levy, & Holmes, 2011).

From a problem-focused perspective, negative imagery can be removed or transformed, whereas from an SF perspective, positive imagery can be created or enhanced. For example, Vasquez and Buehler (2007) found that *imagining future success* enhances people's motivation to achieve it. A positive image of oneself in the future motivates action by helping people to articulate their goals clearly and develop behaviors that will allow them to fulfill those goals. So the very act of imagining future events not only makes those events seem more likely, but also helps to bring them about.

STORY 4. SPORTS PSYCHOLOGY

Positive imagery is one of the main interventions in sports psychology. Currently, there is little overlap between the sports psychology and CBT imagery literature. In contrast to the CBT literature, imagery research in sports psychology has focused on positive imagery and paid little attention to negative imagery. The impression within the sports psychology literature is that negative imagery is an irritant to be circumvented; in contrast, until recently CBT has paid little attention to the deliberate construction of positive images (Hackmann et al., 2011). The reason for this difference might be that sports psychology, in attempting to help athletes build better performances, never adopted the medical model from the outset.

Metacognitive therapy (MCT; Wells, 1995, 1997) is used in treating *generalized anxiety disorder* (GAD). MCT is not aimed at the content of worrying and doesn't teach ways to control worrying. Wells assumes that it is not the content (referred to as *type-I worrying*) that is causing GAD, but the clients' perceptions of their worrying (metacognitions or beliefs about worrying). Worrying is a coping or safety strategy, based on beliefs about worrying (e.g., "Worrying helps me to be prepared to deal with problems," referred to as *type-II worrying* or *meta-worrying*). However, worrying will be strengthened and used more often and in the long run may result in a greater sensitivity to "danger-related" information. This means that clients start to interpret neutral situations as dangerous and focus on negative aspects of a situation. Worrying also results in thinking of more negative outcomes, each of which may lead to more worrying.

Negative metacognitions are based on negative appraisal: "Worrying is harmful" or "Worrying is uncontrollable." These may lead to increasing feelings of anxiety and fear. *Positive metacognitions* are learned by modeling and reinforcement. If a feared event doesn't occur, clients may attribute this to the act of worrying about it, which leads to the development of beliefs such as "Worrying helps me prevent negative events." Note that the connotation "positive" is different from "positive" in SFBT and Positive CBT (Bannink, 2012a, 2014a), because, in themselves. positive metacognitions are negative.

The goal of *eye movement desensitization and reprocessing* (EMDR; Shapiro, 2001) is to process distressing memories, reducing their influence and allowing clients to develop more adaptive coping mechanisms. EMDR uses a structured eight-phase approach to address the past, present, and future aspects of a traumatic or distressing memory that has been dysfunctionally stored (see Volume 3: Trauma).

Mindfulness-based cognitive therapy (MBCT) combines mindfulness meditation rooted in Buddhist thought and Western CBT. Mindfulness involves paying attention to the moment-to-moment experience, whether it is pleasant, unpleasant, or neutral. It increases an open awareness as well as focused attention and reduces automatic responding. Mindfulness may sever the link between negative thoughts and negative emotions (Davidson et al., 2003).

Compassion-focused therapy (CFT) was developed for clients with high shame and self-criticism. They often find experiencing positive emotions (accepting compassion from others and being self-compassionate) difficult. It is process- rather than disorder-focused, because shame and self-criticism are transdiagnostic processes, linked to a range of psychological disorders, such as anxiety disorders. Skills include the use of imagery, building the compassionate self, and using the sense of a compassionate self to engage with areas of personal difficulty (Brewin et al., 2009; Gilbert, 2010).

Fredrickson (2009) describes a compassion-focused intervention: *loving-kindness meditation*. It aims to evoke *positive emotions*, especially within the context of relationships. It increases feelings of warmth and caring for oneself and others. In a guided imagery, clients direct these warm and tender feelings to a nice person or animal, then to themselves, and then to an ever-widening circle of others (to strangers and finally even to people with whom they have a negative relationship; see Exercise 21, p. 131).

Acceptance and commitment therapy (ACT) differs from CBT in that rather than trying to teach clients to control their thoughts, feelings, sensations, memories and other events, ACT teaches them to just notice, accept, and embrace these events, especially unwanted ones. The premise of ACT is that psychological suffering is usually caused by experiential avoidance, cognitive entanglement, and resulting psychological rigidity that leads to a failure to take needed steps in accord with core values (Hayes, Strosahl, & Wilson, 2003).

Positive psychology (PP) is an academic discipline concerned with understanding positive human thought, feeling, and behavior; an empirical pursuit of systematically understanding psychological phenomena; and finally an applied discipline in which interventions are created and employed. PP consists of a family of constructs such as optimism, hope, self-efficacy, self-esteem, positive emotions, flow, resilience, happiness, and gratitude. PP is the study of what makes life worth living and what enables individuals and communities to thrive. It is the study of the conditions and processes that lead to optimal functioning in individuals, relationships, and work (Bannink, 2009b, 2012b). PP represents the efforts of professionals to help people optimize human functioning by acknowledging strengths as well as deficits, and environmental resources in addition to stressors. The study of mental health is distinct from and complementary to the long-standing interest in mental illness, its prevalence, and its remedies (Keyes & Lopez, 2005). Bannink and Jackson (2011) describe a comparison between PP and SFBT.

A wide range of *pharmacological treatments* is available for anxiety disorders. Numerous medications (e.g., benzodiazepines, tricyclic antidepressants, SSRIs) are effective in reducing symptoms associated with anxiety disorders. Medication by itself can relieve symptoms; however, there are no medications that can produce a full, rich, and meaningful life. Medications for anxiety typically result in faster symptom relief than psychotherapy. Yet medications are not curative in the long term and are quite often associated with higher rates of relapse than psychotherapy.

Psychotherapy, either alone or in combination with medication, has been shown to be effective for the treatment of most psychiatric disorders, as well as for prevention of recurrence. In all populations, the combination of medication and psychotherapy provides the most sustained response.

The SF Approach to Anxiety

Medical diseases are commonly characterized by a deficit, and treatments are designed to target—directly or indirectly—that deficit, so that the patient is cured or at least not hindered by the deficit anymore. The history of psychiatry has been dominated by a similar deficit focus. Treatments have been developed to remove or ameliorate the presumed deficit, even if assumptions on the specific nature of the deficits may often have been speculative. Such a deficit focus applies to models of pharmacological treatments as well as psychotherapeutic ones, such as psychoanalysis or CBT, that aim to solve an underlying conflict or to change maladaptive thinking and behaviors. This focus on deficits has a number of limitations; for example, it may strengthen clients' negative image and reduce their sense of control, leaving them passive recipients of expert care. More important is that the deficit focus in psychiatric research has produced, at best, limited progress in developing more effective treatments since the 1980s (Priebe, Omer, Giacco, & Slade, 2014).

Not all therapeutic models, however, have been developed to target deficits. Instead, a number of models aim to tap into the strengths of clients and utilize their positive personal and social resources. Furthermore, data from 40 years of outcome research in psychotherapy provide strong empirical evidence for privileging the clients' role in the change process (Miller, Duncan, & Hubble, 1997). Clients, not therapists, make therapy work. As a result, therapy should be organized around their resources, perceptions, experiences, and ideas. The most potent factor of successful outcome, clients and their propensities for change, is left out of the medical model in traditional psychotherapy.

The problem-solving model in psychotherapy assumes a necessary connection between a problem and its solution, as in modern medicine. This assumption underlies the field's emphasis on assessing problems before making interventions. De Shazer (1985) and Bakker, Bannink, and Macdonald (2010) state that it is not necessary to start treatment with the assessment of problems. As mentioned earlier, the aim of SFBT is to assist clients in describing a detailed vision of their preferred future, and to direct both clients and therapists toward a deeper awareness of the strengths and resources that clients can use in turning their vision into reality.

EXERCISE 5. THREE QUESTIONS TO BUILD HAPPINESS

The following three questions invite clients to build happiness (Isebaert, 2007). Even though it may be difficult for clients to find out what they feel good about, clients may benefit by repeating this exercise at the end of every day for some weeks or even months.

1. "What did I do today that I feel good about?"
2. "What has someone else done that I'm happy with? Did I react in such a way that this person will perhaps do something like that again?"
3. "What else do I see, hear, feel, smell, taste that I like?"

SF questions for clients suffering from anxiety are:

- "How do/did you cope?"
- "What else have you been through that was difficult, and what helped you then?"
- "Which of the things that helped you then could be useful to you again now?"
- "What will you be doing differently when anxiety/worrying is less of a problem in your daily life?"
- "How could you regain hope that life can get easier in the future?"
- "What did the anxiety not change, and how did you manage that?"
- "What things in your life do you wish to maintain, despite anxiety?"

- "What helps you keep anxiety/worries under control?"
- "On a scale of 10 to 0, where 10 equals you are handling anxiety very well and 0 equals you cannot handle anxiety at all, where are you now?" (and follow-up scaling questions).
- "How do you now/did you manage to sometimes feel safe and have control over your life?"
- "How can you comfort yourself?"
- "Who can comfort you, even if only a little bit?"
- "How will you celebrate your victory over anxiety?"

Clients may also be invited to think about the following questions:

- "If a miracle were to happen in the middle of the night, and I overcame the consequences of the anxiety well enough that I didn't have to come here anymore and I was (relatively) satisfied with my life, what would be different then?"
- "What will I be doing differently when these negative thoughts and feelings are less of a problem in my daily life? What difference will those changes make in my life when they have lasted for a longer period of time (days, weeks, months, years)? What difference will they make in my relationships with important people in my life? What difference will the changes that I've accomplished make for future generations of my family?"
- "What would be the smallest sign that things are better? What difference will that make for me? What will be the next small sign? And the

one after that? How will I be able to tell that I am handling life a little better or that it's a little easier for me?"

Getting rid of unhappiness is not the same as achieving happiness. Getting rid of fear, anger, or depression will not automatically fill you with peace, love, and joy. Getting rid of weaknesses will not automatically maximize your strengths. In traditional book titles, the same problem-focused way of thinking about *avoidance goals* is found, as in "Overcoming Depression" or "Your Route out of Perfectionism."

SFBT is by no means phobic to problems and complaints. Clients are given an opportunity to describe their problems or concerns, to which therapists listen respectfully. But no details about the nature and severity of the problem are asked, and possible causes of the problems are not analyzed. By asking about exceptions to the problem, a form of differential diagnosis may reveal that some disorders can be eliminated (e.g., when a parent is asked about exceptions, it may be revealed that a child who would otherwise be diagnosed with ADHD appears to be able to sit still in the classroom).

Another way of conducting SFBT, granting due acknowledgment, is to first collect all problems and then transform all the problem descriptions into what clients want to see instead. Then the collection of problems is discarded, either by tearing it up, if the problems have been written down, or just ignoring it and working with what clients want different in their lives.

Differences in Approaches to Anxiety

Table 3.1 shows a comparison between the traditional and SF approaches to trauma. It explains how the paradigm shift from the problem-solving to the solutions-building approach is applied in the treatment of anxiety.

TABLE 3.1

Differences in Therapeutic Approaches to Anxiety

Traditional Approaches to Anxiety	The SF Approach to Anxiety
Past- and problem-focused	Future- and solution-focused
Diagnosis before treatment	Stepped diagnosis
Focus on negative emotions	Focus on positive emotions with acknowledgment of negative ones
Term *patient* (medical model)	Term *client* (nonmedical model)
Therapist's theory of change	Client's theory of change
Conversations about what patient doesn't want (the problem)	Conversations about what client wants to have instead of the problem
Deficit model: Patient is viewed as damaged. How is the patient affected by anxiety?	Resource model: Client is viewed as influenced but not damaged, having strengths and resources. How did the client respond to anxiety?

TABLE 3.1 *(Continued)*

Differences in Therapeutic Approaches to Anxiety

Traditional Approaches to Anxiety	The SF Approach to Anxiety
Looking for weaknesses and problems	Looking for strengths and solutions: *success analysis*
Patients are (sometimes) seen as not motivated (resistance)	Clients are seen as always motivated, but their goal may differ from that of the therapist
Reducing problems and negative affect is the goal of treatment	Goals are individualized for each client; increasing positive affect may be the goal of treatment
Therapist confronts	Therapist accepts the client's view and asks, "How is that helpful?"
Conversations about impossibilities	Conversations about possibilities
Therapist is the expert and has special knowledge regarding anxiety to which patient submits; therapist gives advice	Client and therapist both have particular areas of expertise; therapist asks questions to elicit client's expertise
Anxiety is always there	Exceptions to anxiety are always there
Long-term treatment	Variable/individualized length of treatment

Treatment aim is recovery from anxiety (avoidance goal)	Treatment aim is what clients want to have instead of anxiety (approach goal)
Coping mechanisms need to be learned	Coping mechanisms are already present
Big changes are needed	Small changes are often enough
Insight or understanding is a precondition	Insight or understanding often comes during or after treatment; focus is on accountability and action
Feedback (sometimes) from patient at end of therapy	Feedback from client at end of every session
Therapist defines end of treatment	Client defines end of treatment

The SF approach can replace traditional approaches or may be combined with them. As an example, biological treatments seem to be strictly problem-focused. Nevertheless, it makes a difference if clients have the idea that "anxiety will disappear" or that they (in positive terms) will be "energetic, active, and relaxed." An SF approach to pharmacological treatment may consist of inviting clients to give a detailed description of what the first signs of recovery might look like, assuming that the medication takes effect, and how the recovery will further manifest itself. Clients are asked what they themselves can add to the effect of the medication, or what they can do to create an environment in which the medication will have maximum effect in helping them to pull through (Bakker et al., 2010).

From an SF point of view, keeping clients in the *expert position* is important. To help clients regain control, therapists may say, "Some clients were able to make the changes you want without trying to understand why they were feeling this way. Other clients have told me it has been helpful to explore the past. Some clients made the changes they wanted first and addressed the causes of anxiety later. What do you suppose will be most helpful for you?"

Keeping clients in the expert position can also be done by asking what they already know about anxiety treatments or inviting them to find (more) information on the Internet; or by first explaining several treatment possibilities and then inviting clients to reflect on which method they might find most useful for them.

EXERCISE 6. BEIGE AND BLUE

With this exercise, I explain to colleagues, clients, and students the difference between working with a *problem focus* and working with a *solutions focus*. I invite them to look around and find five beige objects. Then I invite someone, before the beige objects are listed, to quickly say which blue objects (or objects of his or her favorite color) he or she just saw. The individual probably didn't see any blue objects, or just one or two. When group members are asked what they need to do to find more blue objects, they say they have to focus on blue, not on beige.

This exercise makes clear how clients see their negative situation. They describe it as *beige*: their life is always beige; they don't want beige; they suffer from beige. By asking what they want to have instead of beige (their favorite color), they can begin to focus on this color as a better alternative to beige. "What does a blue life look like?" (goal). "When are/were there pieces of blue already?" (exceptions). "On a scale where 10 indicates a totally blue life and 0 means a totally beige life, where would you like to end and where are you now on that scale?" "At what point on the scale can we stop therapy?"

One last question to all present is: "What do you need to know about beige to help clients focus on blue (or their favorite color)?" The answer to this question is—often to everyone's amazement—*nothing*.

EXERCISE 7. DIFFERENCES IN FOCUS

Benjamin Franklin stated that every problem is an opportunity in disguise. This is an exercise for noticing differences between a *problem focus* and a *solutions focus*. Sit comfortably, close your eyes, and repeat the following sentence 10 times: "I have a big problem!" Observe what you are experiencing physically and emotionally. Notice the effect that this sentence has on your body and emotions.

Get up, stretch a little, and do the exercise again, this time using a different statement. Sit comfortably again, close your eyes, and then repeat the following sentence 10 times: "I have a big opportunity." Once again, observe the effect on your body and emotions.

SF questions in this chapter are:

18. "How do/did you cope?"
19. "What else have you been through that was difficult, and what helped you then? Which of the things that helped you then could be useful to you again now?"
20. "What will you be doing differently when anxiety/panic/worry is less of a problem in your daily life?"
21. "How could you regain hope that life can get easier in the future?"
22. "What did anxiety *not* change, and how did you manage that? What things in your life do you wish to maintain despite anxiety?"
23. "What helps you keep anxiety under control? On a scale of 10 to 0, where 10 equals that you are handling anxiety very well and 0 equals you can't handle anxiety at all, where are you now?" (and all follow-up scaling questions).
24. "How do you manage to sometimes feel safe and have control over your life?"
25. "How can you comfort yourself? Who can comfort you, even if only a little bit?"

26. "How will you celebrate your victory over anxiety?"
27. "Some clients were able to make the changes you want without trying to understand why they were feeling this way. Other clients have told me it has been helpful to explore the past. Some clients made the changes they wanted first and addressed the causes of the anxiety later. What do you suppose will be most helpful for you?"

In the next chapter, we will look at how to create a context for change to help clients move on from anxiety to their preferred future.

4

Creating a Context
for Change

Introduction

In this chapter, the focus is on creating a context for change to help clients move on from anxiety to their preferred future. It starts with building rapport and creating a positive alliance, a necessary condition of change across all forms of psychotherapy. Acknowledgment and validation of clients' experiences are other prerequisites of the therapeutic process. It is important to let clients know that their points of view and actions have been heard and to normalize and reframe their experiences. Building hope and optimism is also important, because most clients suffering from anxiety go through difficult times before they come to see a therapist and may feel hopeless and pessimistic about possibilities for change.

The Therapeutic Alliance

Psychotherapy starts with building rapport. The alliance represents a positive working relationship between therapists and clients, as well as active and collaborative engagement of all involved. Therapists should make explicit efforts to facilitate the creation of a positive and strong alliance and should also systematically monitor the alliance, rather than relying on a clinical impression (see Chapter 8 and 9). Keep in mind that clients' view of the alliance (and not the therapist's!) is the best predictor of outcome. Attention should be paid to the alliance as soon as therapy begins, because positive early alliance is a good predictor of improvement, while poor early alliance predicts client dropout.

In SFBT, the alliance is a negotiated, consensual, and cooperative endeavor in which therapists and clients focus on (a) exceptions, (b) goals, and (c) solutions. When clients are motivated to change, SFBT calls this a *customer-relationship*. When clients are mandated and have no personal problem to work on, this is called a *visitor-relationship*. Sometimes clients want someone else or something else to change. SFBT calls this a *complainant-relationship*. If therapists are not on the same page as their clients, clients may use the expression *Yes, but*, which therapists often interpret as resistance. *Yes, but* drains energy from the conversation, which soon turns into a discussion that revolves around who is right (see for a detailed description of *yes, but* and *yes, and* in Volume 2: Depression).

Four strategies may be applied in a situation where clients think someone or something else needs to change:

1. Say that you wish you could help them, but that you are not a magician. Say you don't think that anyone is able to change anyone else. So how else might you help them? Or ask clients how this is a problem for them.

2. Ask clients to imagine the other person changing in the desired direction, and what they would then notice different about him or her. Also ask what they would notice different about themselves and what difference that would make to their relationship.

3. Investigate the future if the other is not changing by asking what they can still do themselves.

4. Figure out the hoped-for outcome behind earlier attempts.

EXERCISE 8. COMPLAIN ABOUT A THIRD PERSON

Find a partner for doing this exercise and invite him or her to talk about someone else, a third person (not you!), whom he or she would like to change. Ask this person to talk about the same complaint every time, so you can practice with the four strategies described above. Notice the differences brought about by each strategy. Then change roles. In the role of the client, you can learn a lot from the different types of questions that are asked of you.

CASE 2. WHAT DOES THE REFERRER
WANT TO BE DIFFERENT?

The client's superior has referred him to an SF coach. Both the client and his superior agree that the client isn't performing well because of his social phobia. The alliance turns into a customer-relationship when the coach acknowledges that the superior insisted on a coaching path while the client at first felt hesitant. The client is asked not only what he himself would like to be different in his life and work, but also what he thinks his superior wants to be different and what the latter thinks the client should do in order to do well again. By carrying out his own ideas and the ideas he thinks the superior has, the client manages to get back on track.

Focusing on Change

A focus on change is another prerequisite of the therapeutic process. The most useful way to decide which door can be opened to get solutions is by getting a description of what clients will be doing differently and/or what things will be happening that are different when the problem is solved, thus creating the expectation of beneficial change (De Shazer, 1985).

Therapists are constantly reminding clients that they cannot change other people, only themselves. How ironic, therefore, that therapists are trained to develop a treatment plan and enter sessions with the intention of changing their clients! In SFBT, *the role of therapists* is different. Whereas in traditional forms of psychotherapy, the therapist is the only expert in the room and gives advice on how to solve problems, in SFBT the role is one where therapists ask SF questions (they are *not-knowing*), stay one step behind their clients, and look in the same direction (toward the client's preferred future). Clients are seen as co-experts: They are invited to share their knowledge and expertise. When people believe that their personal qualities can be developed further, then, despite the pain of failure, they don't become pessimistic, because they are not being defined by their failures. Change and growth remain a possibility, opening up pathways to success. Dweck (2006) found that students with a fixed mindset have stronger complaints than students with a *growth mindset* (see Volume 2: Depression).

Acknowledgment and Validation

Empathic understanding is required when clients describe what they find difficult and painful in their lives. Affirmation of the client's perspective is important. Then SFBT moves on to explore what clients want to work toward (approach goal) or what clients do to keep their heads above water. In dealing with emotions, it is useful to acknowledge negative emotions like anger, fear, or sadness and to look for possibilities by saying, "I see that your feelings are very strong about this topic. How would you like to feel instead?"

Clients are often in great distress and generally want to make that known. SF therapists respectfully listen to their story and shift to a more positive conversation as soon as possible. It is a misconception that there can only be acknowledgment if the problem is wholly explored or if clients are afforded every opportunity to expatiate on their view of the problem. Utterances such as "I understand that this must be difficult for you" or "I wonder how you have coped so well" offer acknowledgment and take up considerably less time than having clients describe the entire problem. Asking clients what they have tried so far also offers acknowledgment, since most clients have taken steps to address their problems before therapy. However, SF questions like "What have you tried so far that has been helpful, even just a little bit?" or "What has been helpful in getting you through so far?" invite clients to talk about successes (however small) instead of failures, which is usually the case when only the first part of the first question is asked.

Validation of the clients' point of view is also important: "I am sure you must have a good reason for this." In this way, therapists show that they respect clients' opinions and ideas. At the beginning of the first session, therapists may give clients one opportunity *to say what definitively needs to be said* before switching to what clients want different in their lives. This has become a proven method in SF conflict management (Bannink, 2008b, 2009a, 2010bc).

SF questions to offer acknowledgment and validation are:

- "How do you cope?" or "How do you keep your head above water?"
- "How do you ensure the situation isn't worse?"

STORY 5. ACKNOWLEDGE THE PROBLEM

Long ago, the inhabitants of a village were starving because they were afraid of a dragon in their fields. One day a traveler came to the village and asked for food. The villagers explained that they didn't dare to harvest their crops because they were afraid of this dragon. When the traveler heard their story, he offered to slay the dragon, but arriving at the fields, he saw only a large watermelon. He said to the villagers that they had nothing to fear, because there was no dragon, only a watermelon. The villagers were angry at his refusal to understand their fear and hacked him to pieces.

Another traveler came passing by the village, and he too offered to slay the dragon, much to the relief of the villagers. But they hacked him to pieces as well, because he too said they were mistaken about the dragon.

In the meantime, the villagers were desperate, but then a third traveler came to the village. He too promised to kill the dragon. He saw the giant watermelon, reflected for a moment, drew his sword, and hacked the watermelon to pieces. He returned to the village and told the people he had killed their dragon. The traveler stayed in the village, long enough to teach the villagers the difference between dragons and watermelons.

When clients think they need to talk about the problem, they are telling us that they have a *theory of change* about what will help. When the invitation into these problem-saturated conversations is accepted, SF therapists initiate opportunities to help clients identify what changes they hope will result from talking about these experiences (in terms of solutions and goals; George, 2010).

SF questions for clients to ask themselves to *alter their theory of change* are:

- "How will talking about my problems be helpful in making the changes I want?"
- "How will I know that we have talked enough about my problems so we can concentrate on where I would like to go rather than where I've been?"
- "What will be the first signs that will tell me that I am putting the past behind me?"

Normalizing and Reframing

Normalizing depathologizes clients' concerns; it helps them to calm down and realize they're not abnormal for having an anxiety disorder. Thinking it's not normal to have a problem causes a further problem. People are more compassionate with themselves and experience less negative affect when they see that others have the same problems they have. Normalizing both the problem and the ways in which clients and their environment respond to it is key. Neutral language is essential; accusations, threats, hurtful speech, and other words with negative emotional connotations should be avoided. Normalization also changes the moral judgment of and by other persons, and encourages greater understanding from and of the other.

It is important to keep in mind that clients *are* not the problem, but individuals who *have* a problem. Labels like "borderliner" are best avoided. After all, clients are always more than their diagnosis. Instead of saying "Ann is a borderliner" say "Ann has a borderline personality disorder." O'Hanlon and Rowan (2003) also emphasize the importance of distinguishing between person and illness and of examining the effects of the illness on the person. Ask not what disease the person has, but rather what person the disease has.

SFBT proves useful for clients who feel *suicidal* and/or are in *crisis* (see Volume 2: Depression). Clients often benefit from regaining confidence in their competencies and a future-oriented approach. Invite clients to think about their *coping in crisis situations*:

- "How did I manage to get out of bed this morning? Compared to other (bad) days, what did I do differently that helped me get up and come here?"
- "How have I been able to hold on long enough to come here?"
- "How did I manage for so long without seeking professional help?"
- "What am I doing to take care of myself in this situation?"

- "What is the most important thing to remember to continue to cope with this situation?"
- "If 10 equals feeling very well and 0 equals feeling very anxious, where would I like to be?" (and further scaling questions).
- "What would I like to be different when this is over?"
- "How will I/others notice that I have overcome the crisis?"
- "Suppose I look back 1 year, 5 years, or 10 years from now. What will I see that has helped me emerge from this crisis?" or "Suppose that 1 year, 5 years, or 10 years from now I look back together with a friend. What do both of us say I have done in the preceding year(s) that has helped me come out of this so well?"

When clients are *suicidal*, ask them SF *coping questions*:

- "Suppose a miracle happens tonight and you can cope well with this situation, but you are unaware that the miracle has happened because you were asleep. What will you notice first thing tomorrow morning that shows you that the miracle has happened? What else will be different? When the miracle occurs, what will take the place of your pain and your thoughts of killing yourself?"
- "When was the last time you ate something? How did you manage to do that? How did that help you?" "When was the last time you slept? How did you manage to do that? How did that help you?"
- "What helped in the past, even if only marginally?"
- "How do you succeed in getting from one moment to the next?"

- "How will you get through the rest of the day?"
- "Is there anyone else who shares this with you? How is that helpful?"
- "What do your friends or family say you do well, even in very bad times?"
- "Some clients depend on others for hope, because they feel hopeless and must rely on borrowed hope—hope that others hold out for them. What are important people in your life hoping for? What are their best hopes for you?"

Focusing on what clients (and important others) have done to help recovery or prevention in past experiences is useful. When prevention plans fail or are not put into practice, a *recovery plan* may be mapped out, especially with clients who have severe mental problems. This can usually be derived from inviting clients to think about what happened as they regain equilibrium after a previous crisis or hospitalization:

- "What did I do when I started to feel better again?"
- "What usually happens when I begin to emerge from one of my depressive episodes?"
- "What did I learn from previous crises/hospitalizations that may be helpful in this situation?"

For exceedingly pessimistic clients who are often in crisis, predicting the next crisis as a *homework suggestion* may be useful. The therapist asks for details about the next crisis: who will be involved, where it will take place, what effect it will have on others. This may help break a pattern as the therapist and client look for ways to withstand the crisis: how the client solved a previous crisis, what worked before, and what could be used again.

Building Hope

The mere willingness to take part in a conversation with a therapist generates hope and a positive expectancy. These are strengthened when clients' attention is directed toward their options rather than their limitations. When therapists steer clients' attention to their previous successes instead of failures, a further positive expectancy is generated. The notion of the client's personal control is emphasized and problems may be placed outside the client, which serves to remove blame from him or her. If, however, therapists have no confidence in their ability to help clients reach their goals and have lost hope of a favorable outcome, they should examine what is needed to regain hope. Or they should turn clients over to a more hopeful colleague. It is often the assumptions, the attitude, and the behavior of therapists themselves that lead to hopeless cases (see Chapter 8).

STORY 6. DESPAIR AND HOPE

There are two basic responses to hardship: despair and hope. In despair, negativity is multiplied. Fear and uncertainty turn into stress, which can change into hopeless sadness or shame. Despair smothers all forms of positivity, and connections with others are lost. Hope is different. It is not the mirror reflection of despair. Hope acknowledges negativity with clear eyes and kindles positivity, allowing people to connect with others. Hope opens the gateway to bounce back from hardship and emerge even stronger and more resourceful than before. Hope is the belief that the future will be better than today (this belief is the same as in optimism; see Volume 2: Depression) *and* the belief that an individual can influence this.

Frank and Frank (1991, p. 132) looked at the elements of hope in medical treatments.

> Hopelessness can retard recovery or hasten death, while mobilizing hope plays an important part in many forms of healing. Favorable expectations generate feelings of optimism, energy, and wellbeing and may actually promote healing, especially of those illnesses that have a large psychological or emotional component.

More SF questions about hope and optimism are described in Volume 2: Depression. SF questions for *building hope* are:

- "What are your best hopes? What difference will that make?"
- "What has kept your hope alive during this period of difficulty?"

- "Suppose you had a bit more hope. How will your life/relationship be different?"
- "What is the smallest difference that will increase your hope?"
- "When did you feel (more) hopeful, and how did you manage to feel that way?"
- "On a scale of 10 to 0, where 10 equals lots of hope and 0 equals no hope at all, where would you like to be?" (and follow-up scaling questions).
- "What would someone who has (more) hope do in your situation?"
- "What or who can give you more hope?"
- "What indicates that you are on the right track to get over this problem?"
- "Suppose the positive moments were to last longer. What difference will that make for you? How will that increase your hope?"
- "What good things should happen in your life to give you hope that you can leave the bad times behind?"
- "If you want your hope to increase by the next session, what will you do or want me to do before we see each other again?"
- "What in our conversation has given you more hope, even if only a little bit?"

Hope usually grows slowly. Invite clients to *predict* their behavior for the following day and to discover that exceptions to the problem can be found and that more control may be exerted than they probably thought.

Another way to install hope is to ask about *pretreatment change* (Weiner-Davis, de Shazer, & Gingerich, 1987). "Many clients notice that, between the time they call for an appointment and the first session, things already seem different. What have you noticed about your situation?" or "Since you made the appointment and our session today, what is better (even just a little bit)?" "What are these positive changes saying about you as a person?" Scheduling an appointment may help set the wheel of change in motion and present the possibility for an emergent story of competence and mastery. This is consistent with the SF supposition that everything is subject to change and that the point is not to find out *whether* useful change takes place but *when* useful change takes or has taken place.

Imagining a *best possible self* is useful in goal-setting and building hope and optimism. For 20 minutes on four consecutive days, participants in a study done by King (2001) were asked to write down their ideal future, in which all had gone well and they had met their hopes and goals (see Exercise 9). Another group was asked to write about a traumatic experience for those minutes on four consecutive days. Yet another group was asked to write about their ideal future as well as the trauma. The last group was asked to just write about their plans for the day on those four days. The results were that writing about life goals was significantly less upsetting than writing about trauma and was associated with a significant increase in well-being. Five months after writing, a significant interaction emerged such that writing about the trauma or about the best possible self were both associated with decreased illness compared to the other two groups.

EXERCISE 9. BEST POSSIBLE SELF

Invite clients to imagine a future in which they are bringing their *best possible self* forward. Ask them to visualize a best possible self that is very pleasing to them and whom they are interested in. Also ask them to imagine that they have worked hard and succeeded at accomplishing their life goals. You might think of this as the realization of their dreams and their best potential. The point is not to think of unrealistic fantasies, but rather things that are positive and attainable. After they get a clear description, invite them to write the details down. Writing their thoughts and hopes down will help them to envision concrete, real possibilities.

SF questions in this chapter are:

28. "How is this a problem for you?"
29. "I see that your feelings are very strong about this topic. How would you like to feel instead?"
30. "What has been helpful in getting you through so far?" or "What helped in the past, even if only marginally?"
31. "How do you cope?" or "How do you keep your head above water?"
32. "How do you ensure the situation isn't worse than it is?"
33. "Suppose a miracle happens tonight and you can cope with this situation, but you are unaware that the miracle has happened because you

were asleep. What will you notice first thing tomorrow morning that shows you that the miracle has happened? What else will be different?" and "When this miracle occurs, what will take the place of your pain (and the thoughts of killing yourself)?"

34. "How do you succeed in getting from one moment to the next?" or "How will you get through the rest of the day?"

35. "Is there anyone else who shares this with you? How is that helpful?"

36. "What do your friends or family say you do well, even in very bad times?"

37. "Some clients depend on others for hope, because they feel hopeless and must rely on *borrowed hope*—hope that others hold out for them. What are important people in your life hoping for? What are their best hopes for you?"

38. "What are your best hopes? What difference will that make?"

39. "What has kept your hope alive during this period of difficulty?"

40. "Suppose you had a bit more hope. How will your life/relationship be different? What is the smallest difference that will increase your hope?"

41. "When did you feel (more) hopeful, and how did you manage to feel that way?"

42. "On a scale of 10 to 0, where 10 equals lots of hope and 0 equals no hope at all, where would you like to be?" (and follow-up scaling questions).

43. "What would someone who has (more) hope do in your situation?"

44. "What or who can give you more hope?"

45. "What indicates that you are on the right track to get over this problem?

Suppose the positive moments were to last longer. What difference will that make for you? How will that increase your hope?"

46. "What good things should happen in your life to give you hope that you can leave the bad times behind?"

47. "If you want your hope to increase by the next session, what will you do or like me to do before we see each other again?"

48. "What in our conversation has given you more hope, even if only a little bit?"

49. "Many clients notice that, between the time they call for an appointment and the first session, things already seem different. What have you noticed about your situation?" or "Since you made the appointment and our session today, what is better (even just a little bit)?" "What are these positive changes saying about you as a person?"

In the next chapter, we will see how the invitation to describe their preferred future helps clients to focus on possibilities rather than on problems.

5

Describing the Preferred Future

Introduction

Lao Tze stated that vision without action is but a dream, that action without vision is a waste of energy, but that a vision with action can move mountains. The good news is that we can edit the stories about our preferred future. The invitation to describe a new life (vision) and the steps to get there (action) emphasizes the possibility of change.

Setting a goal helps to impose structure on treatment. It makes explicit that therapy will be ended when the goal is achieved, or will be discontinued if there is little or no progress. It also provides the opportunity for an evaluation of outcome. This chapter explains how to set a well-defined goal by inviting clients to give a detailed description of their preferred future, often using future-oriented techniques.

Clients may also be invited to change their perspective, which can be done in several ways: using relationship questions, using the third-person perspective, and externalizing the problem. Changing the meaning of what has happened and using a spiritual perspective are described in Volume 3: Trauma. Once clients have described their new lives, an assessment of motivation, hope, and confidence can be made.

STORY 7. THE CHESHIRE CAT

The Cheshire Cat is a fictional cat popularized by Lewis Carroll's depiction of it in Alice's Adventures in Wonderland (1865). The cat is known for its distinctive mischievous grin. Alice encounters the Cheshire Cat outside on the branches of a tree, where it appears and disappears at will.

Alice: Would you tell me, please, which way I ought to go from here?
The Cat: That depends a good deal on where you want to get to.
Alice: I don't much care where.
The Cat: Then it doesn't much matter which way you go.

Setting a Well-Defined Goal

In problem-focused therapies, it is assumed that the problem is blocking clients from being able to move forward toward their goal. It is assumed that once the problem is solved, clients can move forward in a more productive direction. The way that clients and therapists typically agree to know that the problem is solved is when the problem is reduced or gone: Clients are no longer depressed, or no longer use drugs or alcohol. However, if psychotherapy focuses solely on the reduction of the undesired situation (avoidance goal), clients may not yet have replaced it with the desired situation (approach goal). Finishing therapy at a point where something is not happening rather than at a point when the preferred future is happening involves a greater risk of relapse. The majority of SF conversations focus on three interrelated activities (De Shazer, 1991):

1. Producing exceptions—examples of the goal(s) in clients' lives that point to desired changes
2. Imagining and describing clients' new lives
3. Confirming that change is occurring, that is, that clients' new lives have indeed started

---

CASE 3. TAXI DRIVER

My work is comparable to that of a *taxi driver*. Clients define the destination of the taxi ride (the goal) and it is my responsibility to drive them safely there, ensuring that the route is as short as possible and the ride is comfortable. My first question—as a taxi driver—is: "Where to?" instead of: "Where from?" If clients answer: "Not the airport" (I don't want this problem), I ask them where they like to go instead (Bannink & McCarthy, 2014).

Twelve suggestions for *setting a well-defined goal* include the following:

1. Well-defined goals are phrased as a positive representation, in a process form, in the here-and-now (which means clients can start the solution[s] immediately), as specifically as possible, as being within the client's control, and in the client's language.

   Beijebach (2000) found that setting a well-defined goal in psychotherapy predicts a twofold increase in success. Specific questioning may help to focus clients on *positive targets*. For example, a client said that she wanted to "stop being irritable all the time," and she was asked, "What would you do differently if you were not irritable?" Another SF question would be, "What would you like to be instead of being irritable?"

STORY 8. THE SUPERMARKET

If you go to the supermarket, do you make a list of the things you don't want to buy? This would mean making a list of about 5,000 things you don't want to buy. Of course you'll make a list of what you do want. For that same reason, ask clients what they do want instead of what they don't want.

---

2. Goals should be as *specific* as possible. Clients are often aware in general terms of how they would like to be. For example, a client replied that she wanted "to be normal." The therapist said, "Being normal means

different things to different people. When you feel normal, how will you be different from how you are now? What will tell you that you are normal? What will you be doing that you are not doing now?" Or ask a client who is lacking in self-confidence, "How will you/others know your self-confidence has improved? What will you be doing that you are not doing now?" If possible, goals should be phrased so that more than one person could agree if the goal was achieved, as this is likely to increase the reliability of measures related to goal achievement.

3. Therapists should obtain a detailed *description* of what life looks like and what clients will be doing (differently) when they have reached their goal.

4. Problems can be solved; facts or disabilities cannot be solved. Therefore, it is important to differentiate between problems and disabilities. Solutions can be found for problems; with disabilities (e.g., schizophrenia, autism, intellectual disabilities), individuals and their environment have to adapt in the best possible way. This may influence how far clients can go.

5. Whenever possible, wishes and complaints should be phrased as a goal, that is, as something about which something can be done.

6. Goals are not fixed or static, but can rather be seen as a desired situation. They develop during the process, are refined, and may even change. Goals are not set to achieve an ideal state, but instead to reach a situation that is good or *good enough* from the client's perspective.

7. Clients themselves are not the only ones to define the changes they seek to achieve in their life. Partners, children, colleagues, and referrers

can be asked the same kind of questions about their goal and/or what they see as the goal for the client.

8. Setting an agenda is commonly used in psychotherapy. In SFBT, setting an agenda may also be used, but a question about goal formulation for each item is added: "What will be the best result of discussing this item?" or "How will we know we can stop talking about this item?" (Bannink, 2012a).

9. Whenever possible, invite clients to formulate a *stretch goal*. Stretch goals are goals beyond the client's current performance level (clients have to stretch to reach them). Stretch goals energize clients, who reach for what might appear to be impossible at first and often actually do the impossible. Even when clients don't quite make it, they will probably wind up doing better than they would have done otherwise.

10. In Chapter 4, the method of assessing clients' motivation to change and how change can be encouraged is discussed. In this process, therapists assess the type of alliance they have with clients to optimize cooperation.

11. Invite clients to get started. Ask them to break up the goal into manageable subgoals and enlist the support of others. Check from time to time to see whether clients should modify their goal or abandon it when it no longer serves them. Sometimes the goal should be renegotiated during treatment, but this should be done explicitly, together with clients, thus reducing the risk that they are pursuing different goals.

12. Invite clients to celebrate successes, the conclusion of therapy, and/or victory over anxiety (see Chapter 9).

STORY 9. WINNIE-THE-POOH AND SUCCESS

Different people define *success* in different ways. More and more it has become synonymous with money and status. Real success, however, is less about results or a bottom line and more about the process of achieving goals and dreams. It is not only humans who think that building success is important, but also some animals consider it to be *the most important subject of all. In Winnie-the-Pooh on Success* (Allen & Allen, 1997, p. 17), the wise Stranger tells the animals how they can become successful. He writes the following acronym on a sheet of paper and shows it to his friends:

Select a Dream

Use Your Dreams to Set a Goal

Create a Plan

Consider Resources

Enhance Skills and Abilities

Spend Time Wisely

Start! Get Organized and Go

SF questions for *setting a goal* are:

- "What is the purpose of your visit?"
- "What will be the best outcome of your coming to see me?"

- What will indicate to you/others that you don't need to come here anymore?"
- "What would you/others like to see different as a result of these sessions?"
- "What are your best hopes? What difference will it make when your best hopes are met?"
- "Suppose you're asleep tonight and a miracle happens. The miracle is that the problem that brings you here has been solved (to a sufficient degree). You are unaware of this, because you are asleep. What will you notice first thing tomorrow morning that tells you that the miracle has happened? What will be different? What will you be doing differently? How else will you/others notice over the course of the day that the miracle has happened? How else? How will others react differently?"
- "What would your life look if you were not anxious?"
- "Who would you be without anxiety?"
- "Suppose there was a miracle pill with only positive side effects. How would your life be different?"
- "What impossible goal could you reach if you completely ignored your limitations?"
- "How will you know it has been useful to come here (today)?"
- "Even though it wasn't your idea to come here, what would tell you that it hasn't been a complete waste of time?"
- "Imagine that you take back control of your life from the anxiety. How will you know that you are living a life that does you justice?"

- "Suppose we are a few months ahead from now and these sessions have been useful. How will you notice they have been useful?"
- "If you were to make a mental picture of a situation in the life you desire that you are still avoiding now or that still causes you to experience fear, what would that picture look like?"

Future-Oriented Techniques

SFBT invites clients to give a detailed description of their new lives by doing some *therapeutic time traveling*. Future-oriented techniques use their inner wisdom; clients usually already know the solution(s) to the problem, only they do not know (yet) that they know.

Erickson (Rossi, 1980) was one of the first psychotherapists to use future-oriented techniques, called *pseudo-orientation in time*. During hypnosis, he had clients imagine running into him in six months and telling him that the problem had been solved and how they had achieved that. And even though they did not always apply the same solutions that they had put forward, it turned out that many of them reported doing better six months later.

EXERCISE 10. LETTER FROM YOUR FUTURE

Invite clients to write a letter *from* their future self *to* their current selves from X years from now (6 months, 1 year, 5 years, or maybe 10 years, whichever is for them a relevant period of time; Dolan, 1991). Ask them to describe that they are doing fine, where they are, what they are doing, and what crucial things they did to get there. Finally ask them to give their present selves some sage and compassionate advice from the future.

Another future-oriented technique, *older and wiser self,* invites clients to imagine that many years later they are an *older and wiser version of themselves* (Dolan, 1991). They are still healthy and have all their intellectual capabilities. Clients may even go for a walk with the older and wiser version and ask for advice regarding their problem:

- "What would this older and wise person advise me to do in order to get through the present phase of my life? "
- "What would this person say that I should be thinking of?"
- "What would this person say that would help me the best to recover from anxiety and function well (again)?"
- "What would this person say about how I could console myself?"
- "How, from this person's view, could therapy (if needed) be most useful to me?"

STORY 10. POSITIVE VISUALIZATION

Positive visualization refers to the practice of seeking to affect the outer world by changing one's thoughts and expectations. Athletes frequently use positive visualization to enhance their performance. Some celebrities have claimed that visualization had a significant role in their success. Such celebs include Oprah, Tiger Woods, Arnold Schwarzenegger, Anthony Robbins, and Bill Gates. Actor Jim Carrey wrote a check to himself in 1987 in the sum of 10 million dollars. He dated it Thanksgiving 1995 and added "for acting services rendered." He visualized it for years, and in 1994 he received $10 million for his role in *Dumb and Dumber*.

Clients may profit from positive visualization as much as athletes and celebrities do.

EXERCISE 11. LIFE SUMMARY

Invite clients to write a description of how they would like to have their life relayed to their grandchildren (or a young child whom they care about). A few days later, ask them to review the summary and take stock in what is missing in their life and which changes are needed to make the summary a reality.

A variation of the life summary is to write a *eulogy*: "How do I want to be remembered?" A eulogy is a piece written in praise of a person who recently died or retired. Covey (1989) uses a similar technique: One of the habits of "highly effective people" is *to begin with the end in mind*. This means to start with a clear understanding of your destination. It means to know where you are going so that the steps you take are always in the right direction. One of the ways to do so is to imagine attending your own funeral in three years' time. What difference would you like your family, friends, and colleagues to say you have made in their lives?

_____

_____

EXERCISE 12. ONE YEAR LATER

Invite clients to describe in detail a day in their life one year in the future. If clients have difficulty in making a choice between two alternatives, this can be a good intervention, as the consequences of both choices become apparent. Even if therapists have the impression that clients don't discern the consequences of a certain choice, it can still be a valuable intervention.

_____

_____

EXERCISE 13. FIVE-YEAR PLAN

Invite clients to look further ahead than usual. Ask them to divide a large sheet of paper into fields. On the vertical lines, ask them to list subgoals they would like to reach (e.g., work, family, friends, and leisure; see Figure 5.1). On the horizontal lines, have them write down 1 year through to 5 years from now. In the fields, the clients write the steps they will take to reach their goal, starting with the situation five years from now and then working backward. "If that's where I want to be in five years, how far do I need to have come four years from now? Three years from now? What should I have achieved by then? Two years from now? One year?" The five-year plan helps clients formulate realistic goals and lay them out on a timeline to illuminate what steps they can take to maximize the chances of reaching their goals in five years' time.

FIGURE 5.1
The Five-Year Plan

Goals	1 year	2 years	3 years	4 years	5 years
Work					
Family					
Leisure					

EXERCISE 14. COMIC STRIP

A *comic strip*, a sequence of interrelated drawings in panels to form a narrative, is another way to define the goal and the steps to get there (Figure 5.2). As most children are animal lovers, ask them which animal they would like to be in the future and which animal they compare themselves to now. Ask them to draw a comic strip with six drawings, first drawing the animal they want to be (e.g., a lion, field

6), then drawing the animal they are now (e.g., a mouse, field 1). Then have the children draw the other pictures (drawings 2 through 5) in any order they wish. Also ask children which strengths and resources of the animal in the first field they want to take with them as they transform into the preferred animal. Discuss the drawings with the children (and their parents) and translate the drawings to their life as a child. The comic strip technique is also used in SFBT with adults and in team coaching, always starting with the last drawing.

FIGURE 5.2

Comic Strip

1	2	3
4	5	6

EXERCISE 15. START AT CHAPTER TWO.

Say, "A book is made up of many chapters. You can see your life in this way. If you were to write the story of your life, begin with the second chapter instead of Chapter One. All the problems and anxiety, which you are currently experiencing, can be omitted. What positive differences would there be in your life description? Which people would you omit, and which would you include to make them part of Chapter Two? Which strengths and resources do you have in Chapter Two? Which good ideas from Chapter Two could you be already using?" As an exercise, write your own life story, but begin at Chapter Two.

Using Different Perspectives

Inviting clients to change their perspective can be done in several ways. Clients may be invited to change the meaning of what happened or use a spiritual perspective (see Volume 3: Trauma). Descriptions of interactional events and their meaning can also be constructed by asking relationship questions. Another way to change perspective is to externalize the problem: Clients are invited to see the problem as something separate from themselves that affects them, but doesn't always control every aspect of their lives. Yet another way is to use the third-person perspective.

When using *relationship questions*, therapists find out who are the clients' significant others and weave them into the questions to encourage clients to describe their situations and what they want different in interactional terms. "Supposing the two of you got along better in the future, what would your husband notice you doing instead of losing your temper?" or "What will your children say will be different when things are better between the two of you?"

Walter and Peller (1992) introduced the *interactional matrix*, a tool for building solutions from an interactional view to invite clients into areas of difference (see Figure 5.3). Across the top of the matrix are the following frames: goal, hypothetical solutions, and exceptions. Along the left side of the matrix are the different reporting positions. The first is the *for self* position. Questions from this position invite clients to answer from their own point of view. The next position is *for the other*. Questions from this position invite clients to answer questions as if they were listening and reporting for someone else. In order to answer these questions, clients have to suspend their own way of thinking and imagine the other(s) answering the question. They have to put themselves in the other's shoes or at least think of what the other person might say if he or she were responding to the question.

The third row of the matrix reports from a *detached position (observer)*. This position is of someone who is observing: "If I were a fly on the wall observing you and your partner, what will I see you doing differently when things are better?" or "Imagine that you consulted someone about your situation, someone you highly respect, who may not even be alive today, or whom you may not know personally. What would that person advise you to do or think?" Each question or row of the matrix invites clients into an area of experience different from their usual way of thinking.

FIGURE 5.3 **Interactional Matrix**			
Position	**Goals**	**Hypothetical solutions**	**Exceptions**
Self			
Other			
Observer			

EXERCISE 16. SELF, OTHER, AND OBSERVER

Ask clients these *relationship questions* using the same three perspectives (self, other, and observer). Especially in cases where clients want someone else to change, these questions may be useful. Note that the question starts with "when" instead of "if," suggesting that the problem will (eventually) disappear (see Chapter 2).

1. "When this problem is solved, what will you notice that is different about the other person? What will you see him/her doing differently? What else?"

2. "When this problem is solved, what will this other person notice that is different about you? What will this other person see you doing differently? What else?"

3. "When this problem is solved and an outside observer is watching you, what will he/she notice that is different about your relationship with the other person? What will this observer see both of you doing differently? What else?"

Externalizing the problem helps clients change perspective and see the problem as something separate from themselves that affects them, but doesn't always control their lives. This intervention comes from *narrative therapy* (White & Epston, 1990). With externalization of the problem, clients are free to separate themselves from their problematic self-image. The problem is seen as something that lies outside themselves and has a negative influence on them but does not define them. Clients first give a name to the problem like *Fear, Stress,* or *Worries*—a noun (X) is best for this. "How would you name the problem that bothers you?" Then questions are asked about exceptions: times when the problem (X) is not there or is less noticeable, and what clients do to bring that about. Clients are invited to talk about the times when X is present and how they succeed in coping with it. Depending on their needs, more or less time can be spent on finding out how X controls their lives. Their competencies are highlighted, increasing their confidence that more control is possible. Also, the tendency to apportion blame for the problem to other(s) is minimized. During each session, clients indicate on a scale of 10 to 0 the extent to which X has control over them: 10 equals they have complete control over X, and 0 equals X has complete control over them. It is apparent that in most cases the problem may disappear as control over X increases.

SF questions for *externalizing the problem* are:

- "What would you name the problem that bothers you?"
- "At what point on the scale 10 to 0 are you today?" If the point is higher than the last session: "How did you succeed in doing that?" If the point is the same as the last session: "How did you manage to maintain the same point?" If the point is lower than the last session: "What did you do earlier on to go ahead again? What have you done in the past in a similar situation that has been successful? What have significant others in your life noticed about you in the last week? How did that influence their behavior toward you?"
- "What do you do (differently) when you have (more) control over X?"
- "What do you do when you attack X? Which weapons help the most?"
- "How are you able to fool or deceive X?"
- "How will you celebrate your victory over X?"
- "How long has X had you in its grip?"
- "Which people, who have known you when you were not ill, can remind you of your strengths, your accomplishments, and that your life is worth living?"

- "When X (Anxiey, Panic) whispers in your ear, do you always listen?"
- "What can you tell me about your past that would help me understand how you have been able to stand up to X (Anxiety/Panic) so well?"

Using the *third-person perspective* is another way to change perspective.

A common goal of therapy is to change the self, so clients should be particularly interested in assessing how they have changed since beginning treatment. Assessing change matters because it constitutes critical determinants of satisfaction and well-being (Carver & Scheier, 1998) and also guides future courses of action: "Am I becoming less anxious?" or "Are we doing better in our relationship?"

Self-change influences people's memory perspective. *Third-person recall* produces judgments of greater self-change when people are looking for evidence of change, but lesser self-change when they are looking for evidence of continuity. Ross and Wilson (2002) found that recalling an old, pre-change self from the third-person perspective helps to deal with maintaining change. Greater perceived change leads to greater satisfaction with one's efforts and, therefore, makes it easier to summon the resources necessary to maintain one's efforts.

Libby, Eibach, and Gilovich (2005) found that there are two ways of seeing oneself as successful: from the first-person and the third-person perspective. There is a much greater chance of continuing with desired behavior when one considers oneself from a third-person perspective. This theory builds on the research showing that we interpret the behavior of others as being indicative of their personality, whereas we interpret our own behavior as being indicative of the situation we are in. Therefore, seeing ourselves from the third-person perspective allows us to see the sort of person who engages in that sort of behavior. Seeing oneself as the type of person who would engage in a desired behavior increases the likelihood of engaging in that behavior.

Vasquez and Buehler (2007) found that people feel more motivated to succeed on a future task when they visualize its successful completion from a third-person rather than a first-person perspective. Actions viewed from the third-person perspective are generally construed at a relatively high level of abstraction—in a manner that highlights their larger meaning and significance—which heightens motivational impact. They found that students experience a greater increase in achievement motivation when they imagine their successful task completion from a third-person rather than from a first-person perspective. Moreover, research shows that third-person imagery boosts motivation by prompting people to perceive it as important.

Assessing Motivation, Hope, and Confidence

It would be nice if clients and therapists began therapy with the assumption that it is being used as intended: to find solutions or to put something behind them. However, not all clients see themselves as being part of the problem and/or solutions. In those cases, traditional psychotherapies use the concepts of resistance and noncompliance. Resistance implies that clients don't want to change and that therapists are separate from the client system they are treating. However, it is more helpful to see clients as cooperating: They are showing therapists how they think change takes place. As therapists understand their thinking and act accordingly, there is always cooperation. If therapists see resistance in the other person, they cannot see their efforts to cooperate; if, on the other hand, they see their unique way of cooperating, they cannot see resistance. Each client should be viewed from a position of therapist–client cooperation, rather than from a focus on resistance, power, and control (De Shazer, 1984, p. 13). Clients who don't carry out the homework don't demonstrate resistance, but are actually cooperating because in that way they are indicating that this homework is not in accordance with their way of doing things. It is the therapist's task to assist clients in discovering their competencies and using them to create the preferred future.

With resistance as a central concept, therapist and client are like opposing tennis players. They are engaged in fighting against each other, and the therapist needs to win in order for the therapy to succeed. With cooperation as a central concept, therapist and client are like tennis players on the same side of the net. Cooperating is a necessity, although sometimes it becomes necessary to fight alongside your partner so that you can cooperatively defeat your mutual opponent.

Also in Erickson's view (Rossi, 1980), resistance is cooperative: It is one of the possible responses clients make to interventions.

One of the principles of *motivational interviewing* (Miller & Rollnick, 2002) is unconditional acceptance of the client's position. Therapists build a relationship that is based on collaboration, individual responsibility, and autonomy. Miller and Rollnick stated that the necessity of approaching clients in a nonmoralizing way is impeded if therapists are unprepared or unable to defer their own (mistaken) ideas about problem behavior. Therapists should react with empathy, avoid discussions, and strengthen clients' self-efficacy. Miller and Rollnick describe *change talk*. This is a method of SF communication for enhancing clients' intrinsic motivation to change by stressing the advantages of the behavior change. To elicit change talk, they ask open-ended questions, such as "How would you like to see things change?" or "How would you want your life to look in five years' time?"

SF questions in this chapter are:

50. "What would you do differently if you were not irritable?" or "What would you like to be instead of being irritable?"
51. "Being normal means different things to different people. When you feel normal, how will you be different from how you are now? What will tell you that you are normal? What will you be doing that you are not doing now?"
52. "How will you/others know your self-confidence has improved? What will you be doing that you are not doing now?"

53. "What will be the best result of discussing this item?" or "How will we know we can stop talking about this item?"

54. "What is the purpose of your visit?" or "What will be the best outcome of your coming to see me?" or "What will indicate to you/others that you don't need to come here anymore?" or "What would you/others like to see different as a result of these sessions?"

55. "Suppose you're asleep tonight and a miracle happens. The miracle is that the problem that brings you here has been solved (to a sufficient degree). You are unaware of this, however, because you are asleep. What will you notice first thing tomorrow morning that shows you that the problem has been solved? What will be different? What will you be doing differently? How else will you notice over the course of the day that the miracle has happened? How else? How will others notice that the miracle has occurred? How will they react differently?"

56. "How would your life look if you were not anxious?"

57. "Suppose there was a miracle pill with only positive side effects. How would your life be different?" or "What *impossible* goal could you reach if you completely ignored your limitations?"

58. "How will you know that it has been useful to come here today?"

59. "Even though is wasn't your idea to come here, what would tell you that it hasn't been a complete waste of your time?"

60. "Imagine that you take back control of your life from the anxiety. How will you know that you are living a life that does you justice?"

61. "Suppose we are a few months ahead from now and these sessions have been useful. How will you notice they have been useful?"

62. "If you were to make a mental picture of a situation in your desired life that you are still avoiding now or that still causes you to experience fear, what would that picture look like?"

63. "Supposing the two of you got along better in the future, what would your husband notice you doing instead of losing your temper?" or "What will your children say will be different when things are better between the two of you?"

64. "If I were a fly on the wall observing you and your partner, what will I see you doing differently when things are better?" or "Imagine that you consulted someone about your situation, someone you highly respect, who may not even be alive today, or whom you may not know personally. What would that person advise you to do or think?"

65. "When this problem is solved, what will you notice that is different about the other person? What will you see him/her doing differently? What else? When this problem is solved, what will this other person notice that is different about you? What will this other person see you doing differently? What else? When this problem is solved and an outside observer is watching you, what will he/she notice that is different about your relationship with the other person? What will this observer see both of you doing differently? What else?"

66. "What would you name the problem that bothers you? At what point on the scale of control over X are you today?" (plus all the follow-up scaling questions).

67. "How would you like to see things change?" or "How would you want your life to look in five years' time?"

In the next chapter, we will see that all clients possess strengths and competencies that can help to improve their well-being. Finding competence helps clients discover how they manage to cope, even in the most difficult circumstances.

6

Finding Competence

Introduction

Shining a spotlight on change illuminates clients' existing personal strengths and resources. Erickson (as quoted in Rosen, 1991) describes this as clients' vast storehouse of learning. Focusing on strengths and competence—making a success analysis—increases clients' motivation and helps them to discover how they manage to cope.

Another way to find competence is to find *exceptions*, which clients often overlook. Problems may persist only because clients think or say that the problem "always" occurs. Times when the problem is absent or is less of an issue lie at the surface, but they are dismissed as insignificant or are not even noticed and hence remain hidden. SF therapists keep an eye out for exceptions; they help to shift their clients' attention to those times when things are/were different and through which solutions reveal themselves.

Asking competence questions stimulates clients to talk about successes and positive differences and to give self-compliments, which feeds their feeling of self-worth. Questions about details are key: "What else?" "And what else?" It is important to keep inquiring about everything that looks like a success, a resource, or something that clients value in themselves. Moreover, the question "What else?" implies that there is more and that all clients need to do is find out what it is.

Finding Strengths and Resources

All people have capacities that can be drawn upon to better the quality of their life despite the challenges they face. Therapists should respect these capacities and the directions in which clients wish to apply them. Clients' motivation is increased by a consistent emphasis on strengths as they define them. The discovering of strengths requires a process of cooperative exploration. It turns therapists away from the temptation to judge or blame clients for their difficulties and toward discovering how clients manage(d) to survive and maybe even thrive. All environments—even the most bleak—contain resources. Saleebey (2007) describes this as the strengths perspective.

Masten (2001) found an important distinction between strengths and *resilience*. Strengths refer to attributes of a person, such as good coping abilities, or protective circumstances, such as a supportive partner. Resilience refers to the processes whereby these strengths enable adaptation during times of challenge. Thus, once therapists help clients identify strengths, these strengths can be used to help understand and enhance client resilience (Bannink, 2008a, 2014b).

SFBT gives recognition to the actions clients are or were able to take even though they are or were feeling low. This helps them identify their own unique strengths in making things better. Recognizing themselves as being successful, even in a small way, initiates more positive feelings and a belief that things have been and/or can be better. If clients cannot find any strength, invite them to look at themselves through a more positive lens, using the *third-person perspective* (see Volume 2: Depression and Volume 3: Trauma).

SF questions to invite clients to *find personal strengths* are:

- "What strengths do I/others think I possess to stand up to anxiety?"
- "What is it that gives me the strength to get up in the morning?"
- "How come I have not given up hope?"
- "What might my best friend admire about the way that I have been struggling with this?"
- "What have I done to stop things from getting worse?"
- "What have I managed to hold on to even though things got worse?"
- "What is my approach to finding solutions to tough situations?"
- "What wisdom have I gained from these difficult times that I would like to pass on to people I love or care for (e.g., [grand]children or friends)?"
- "What are some of the things that I have thought, said, or done that have helped me move from where I started to where I am now?"

The key to building a new habit is to practice the behavior, over and over. The famous aikido master Ueshiba states that instructors could impart merely a small portion of the teachings and that people can only through ceaseless training acquire the necessary experience. His advice is to not chase after many techniques, but one by one to make each technique your own. This works for strengths as well. Here are a few ways that resonate for many clients:

- *Survey:* Fill out the VIA (Values in Action) Survey of Character Strengths (www.authentichappiness.org) to find out what your signature strengths are.
- *Conversation:* Talk with others about your strengths; tell stories about how your strengths have helped you and were at play when you were at your best. Use your strengths while you are in conversation; for example, if you want to build upon curiosity, ask questions with a sense of genuine interest.
- *Journaling:* Write about your strengths; explore them in this intrapersonal way. For example, if you want to build upon prudence, consider a situation you are conflicted about, and write about the costs and benefits of both sides.
- *Self-monitoring:* Set up a tracking system to monitor your experiences throughout the day. Track one or more of the strengths you are using hour by hour; you may need an alarm or another external cue to remind yourself to monitor when you use your strengths. This strategy involves using your strength of self-regulation.

CASE 4. COMPETENCE TRANSFERENCE

Lamarre and Gregoire (1999) describe a technique called *competence transference* in which they invite clients to talk about other areas of competence in their lives, such as sports, a hobby, or a special talent. They ask clients to bring those abilities to bear in order to reach their goals. As an example, they describe how a client suffering from a panic disorder learned to relax by applying his knowledge of deep-sea diving whenever he experienced anxiety.

CASE 5. POSITIVE SUPERVISION

"How fragile and uncertain I was, when I got a job as an intern at a mental health institution. My supervisor looked at the mistakes I made and at skills I didn't have (yet). When my imperfections were highlighted, I always had the urge to defend myself. This, however, was like fighting a losing battle: A mistake was a mistake and "I should have known." I cringed and started to feel anxious about the supervision, and I grew more and more uncertain. The last months of my internship, I went to the supervision sessions with abdominal pain.

My experience was very different when I met a supervisor who used a positive focus. I was asked about my goal for the supervision. By using a scale of 10 to 0, we examined how far I was in completing my goals already. I was asked how I was able to give a 6 on the scale and not lower. We examined what competencies I owned and in what situations I managed to act according to my goals. I was surprised; we didn't look at my weaknesses, but rather at my strengths and skills. I suddenly felt a lot more capable in my work than I previously thought I was.

The strict hierarchy with a focus on errors disappears; there is a more equal relationship. Because there is also room for the person of the supervisee, I felt recognized and respected. Personal circumstances or characteristics that complicate working with clients, such as my perfectionism, are also addressed. In this way, supervision becomes a fun part of the training, and experiencing a shared passion creates more meaning in your work. I literally felt the urge to run to the sessions to share with my supervisor new developments and my growth. After enthusiastically sharing a certain technique, she remarked, 'Who do you think was more surprised that it worked out so well, you or your client?'"

EXERCISE 17. YOU AT YOUR BEST

Invite clients to remind themselves of a time when they were at their best. Where were they, who was there with them, and what were they thinking, doing, and feeling? This could be an experience that brings forth pleasant memories, such as a birthday, wedding, job interview, or a time when they accomplished something important. They might find benefit from doing this exercise with physical memorabilia—photos, trinkets collected from a vacation, trophies or awards, meaningful letters, or college degrees. After clients recall the event, invite them to take a few minutes to bask in the past success and pleasant feelings this experience brings forth. Don't ask them to figure out why certain things happened; this is often counterproductive. Instead, invite them to focus on replaying the experience.

This exercise has been shown to build positive emotions and confidence. Another version is to invite clients to imagine themselves *at their best* during an upcoming event, such as an exam, instead of a past event. Or simply ask, "When are you at your best? What does that look like?" or "What was the highest point on the scale from 10 to 0 you have ever been? What did that look like?"

Finding Exceptions

Exceptions are those behaviors, perceptions, thoughts, and feelings that contrast with the problem and have the potential of leading to a solution if amplified by the therapist and/or increased by the client (Lipchik, 1988, p. 4). For clients, the problem is seen as primary, and exceptions, if seen at all, are seen as secondary, whereas for SF therapists, exceptions are seen as primary. Interventions are meant to help clients make a similar inversion, which will lead to the development of a solution (De Shazer, 1991). When asked about exceptions, which are the keys to solutions, clients may start noticing them for the first time. Solutions are often built from unrecognized differences. Wittgenstein (1953/1968) states that exceptions lie on the surface; you don't have to dig for them. However, clients tend to pass them over, because they feel the problem is always happening. These exceptions, which are aspects of events that are very important for us to see, are hidden because of their simplicity and familiarity. According to Wittgenstein, therapists shouldn't excavate, speculate, or complicate. That is why in SFBT, therapists stay on the surface and resist the temptation to categorize or to look for the essence of the problem. It is the task of therapists to help clients find these exceptions and to amplify them, so that these exceptions start to make a difference for them. Two types of exceptions are:

1. *Exceptions pertaining to the goal*: "When do you see glimpses of what you want to be different in your life already? When was the last time you noticed this? What was it like? What was different?"
2. *Exceptions pertaining to the problem*: "When was the problem less severe? When was the problem not there for a (short) period of time? When was there a moment you were able to cope a little bit better?"

If exceptions are deliberate, clients can make them happen again. If exceptions are spontaneous, clients may discover more about them, for example, by monitoring exceptions or trying to predict them (see Exercise

23, p. 137). Therapists, having heard and explored these exceptions, compliment clients for all the things they have done. They invite clients to relate their success stories using three *competence questions*:

1. "How did you do that?"
2. "How did you decide to do that?"
3. "How did you manage to do that?"

The first question assumes that clients have done something and therefore supposes action, competence, and responsibility. The second question assumes that clients have taken an active decision, affording them the opportunity to write a new life story with influence on their future. The third question invites clients to relate their successes.

Exceptions can be found in any symptom within all anxiety disorders.

Invite clients to think about exceptions with the following *exception-finding questions*:

- "When was there a situation where I felt less anxious?"
- "Which days in the past few weeks were somewhat better?"
- "When in the past week was I able to worry less (even just a little bit)?"
- "When in the last few weeks did I feel a bit more relaxed?"
- "How did I overcome the urge to . . . (use alcohol, avoid a difficult situation)?"
- "What happens when the problem ends or starts to end?"
- "When do/did I feel a bit more safe?"

EXERCISE 18. PAY ATTENTION TO WHAT YOU DO WHEN YOU OVERCOME THE URGE

Although clients often say that the problematic behavior (e.g., alcohol or drug use, gambling, self-mutilation, avoidance reaction, obsessive-compulsive behavior) always occurs, there are always circumstances under which the problematic behavior doesn't manifest itself (to the same degree). These are exceptions on which clients can build, because they are already part of their repertoire. This presupposes that clients definitely conquer the urge every now and then and that they are doing something different in order to overcome the urge. Clients' attention is directed to their behavior, not to any interior sensation. It may also be useful to draw attention to how other people overcome their urge in comparable situations.

CASE 6. EXCEPTIONS

As a homework suggestion, the client is invited to notice all exceptions regarding the panic disorder she is suffering from. When does the panic and avoidance that goes with it not manifest itself (to the same degree)? When does she succeed in keeping doing what she is doing, despite panic whispering in her ear? When does she succeed in shortening the panic (even just a little bit)? When does she succeed in preventing the panic attack from happening?

STORY 11. THE BRIGHT SPOTS

This story is about Jerry Sternin, who in the 1990s was working for Save the Children. The Vietnamese government invited the organization to help fight malnutrition in children resulting from huge problems: poverty, ignorance, poor sanitation, and lack of access to clean water. According to Sternin, all these problems were TBU: True But Useless. The millions of kids couldn't wait for those problems to be solved, and he wasn't able to fight these causes. Sternin decided to do something else: He traveled to rural villages and met with the local mothers. They went out to weigh and measure every child in their village. The results were surprising: They found kids who were bigger and healthier than others (the exceptions). Sternin searched for the "bright spots": people whose behaviors created better results than those of their neighbors, using the same resources. The bright-spot mothers fed their kids more meals in a day (using the same amount of food). Healthy kids were also actively fed while unhealthy kids ate on their own. The bright-spot mothers collected shrimp and crabs from the rice fields (considered adult food) and sweet potato greens (considered low-class food) and mixed them with the rice, making the meal more nutritious.

Sternin ensured that the solution would be a native one. He invited the mothers to practice the new behaviors, and they spread to other villages. It was hugely successful: Over the next six months, 65% of the kids were better nourished and stayed that way, and the program reached 2.2 million Vietnamese people in 265 villages.

What is remarkable is that Sternin was no expert and didn't have the answers when he started. But he did have a deep faith in the power of finding exceptions: *the bright spots* (Heath & Heath, 2010).

Scaling Questions

By means of scaling questions, therapists help clients express complex, intuitive observations about their experiences and estimates of future possibilities. Scaling questions invite clients to put their observations, impressions, and predictions on a scale from 10 to 0.

In the SF literature, scaling questions are used in different ways. Therapists mostly work with scales from 0 to 10, sometimes with scales from 1 to 10—the latter presumably because the fact that clients are visiting a therapist already implies some improvement. My clinical impression is that clients give a higher rating if scales from 10 to 0 are used rather than from 0 to 10, which improves their self-perception.

The third of the four basic SF questions is: "What works?" and "What else?" I choose to ask these questions before I ask clients to give a rating on the scale—contrary to the standard use of SFBT, according to which one first asks for a rating and subsequently inquires what the rating means. It is my experience that clients give higher ratings if they are first asked what works (and what else works). This has to do with *cognitive dissonance*: If clients give a low rating on the scaling questions, they don't search much further to find things that work.

Scaling questions focus on progress, motivation, hope, or confidence. They can be asked at the end of the session, when therapists have looked for exceptions or discussed the miracle/goal. Scaling questions may begin with a scenario such as the following: "If the miracle (or another description of the preferred future) equals 10 and the moment when things were at their worst (or the moment you made the appointment) equals 0, where on the scale would you like to end?" Most clients state a 7 or 8. "What will be different at that point?" "What else will be different?" "Where are you now on the scale?" "How do you succeed in being at that point (how is it not lower)?" "What does one point higher look?" "What will you be doing differently?" "How might you be able to move up one point?" "What or who might be helpful?" "At what point do you think you can stop therapy?"

Other scaling questions might be "On a scale of 10 to 0, where 10 equals you are handling the situation very well and 0 equals you can't handle the situation at all, where would you like to be?" and follow-up scaling questions. Or "What is one small thing you/others will notice different in your life which shows you/them that you have moved one step ahead on your path to recovery?"

CASE 7. SCALING QUESTIONS

Say, "Here is a different kind of question, called a *scaling question*, which puts things on a scale from 10 to 0. Let's say 10 equals how your life will be when your best hopes are met and 0 equals the opposite (see Table 6.1). Where on the scale would you like to be (X = realistic aim)? What will be different in your life then? What will you be doing differently? Where are you on the scale today (Y)? How is it not lower than it is? What else have you done? How will one point higher on the scale look? What will be small signs of progress ($Y + 1$)? How will you/others know you are one point higher? What will you be doing differently? Who or what can help you to reach that higher point?"

TABLE 6.1   Scaling Questions

10	Best hopes are met
X	Realistic aim
Y + 1	Small signs of progress or one point higher on the scale
Y	Present situation and "What have you done to reach this point? How come it is not lower that it is? How did you do that? What does it say about you? Who would agree? What else have you done?"
0	Opposite of best hopes

Scaling questions are also frequently used in problem-focused thera-pies. However, these scales are about the problem: a depression scale, an anxiety scale, or an SUD (Subjective Units of Distress) scale in EMDR. On these scales, the highest point is where the problem is at its peak and the 0 is where the problem is absent. However, the absence of the problem doesn't say anything about the presence of positive feelings, thoughts, or behavior, as shown in the previous chapters. In SFBT, a neutral scale replaces an anxiety scale or stress scale, where 10 equals complete relaxation and 0 equals the opposite.

STORY 12. AT THE CAR WASH

A car wash ran a promotion featuring loyalty cards. Every time cus-tomers bought a car wash, their card was stamped, and when they had eight stamps they got a free wash. Other customers got a dif-ferent loyalty card. They needed to collect 10 stamps (rather than eight) to get a free car wash—but they were given a "head start": Two stamps had already been added.

The goal was the same: Buy eight additional car washes and then get a reward. But the psychology was different: In one case, you're 20% of the way toward the goal; in the other case, you're starting from scratch. A few months later, 19% of the eight-stamp customers had earned a free wash, versus 34% of the head-start group (and the head-start group earned the free wash faster; Cialdini, 1984)

So people find it more motivating to be partly finished with a longer journey than to be at the starting gate of a shorter one. To motivate action is to make people feel as though they're closer to the finish line than they might have thought That is why SF therapists always ask, "How come the point on the scale isn't lower than it is?"—thereby putting a few stamps on their clients' car wash cards.

Depression, which often accompanies anxiety, is characterized by negative views of oneself, one's life experience (and the world in general), and the future. In Volume 2: Depression, how to develop a positive view of oneself is described.

SF questions in this chapter are:

68. "What else? And what else?"
69. "When are you at your best? What does that look like?"
70. "What was the highest point on the scale from 10 to 0 you have ever been? What did that look like?"
71. "When do you see glimpses of what you like to be different in your life already? When was the last time you noticed this? What was it like? What was different then?"
72. "When was the problem less severe?" or "When was the problem not there for a (short) period of time?" or "When was there a moment you were able to cope a little bit better?"

73. "How did you do that?" or "How did you decide to do that?" or "How did you manage to do that?"

74. "If the miracle (or another description of the preferred future) equals 10 and the moment when things were at their worst (or the moment when you made the appointment) equals 0, at what number do you think you can stop therapy?"

75. "What is one small thing you/others will notice that's different in your life, showing you/them that you have moved one step ahead on your path to recovery?"

76. "Let's say that 10 equals how your life will be when all is going very well and 0 equals how bad things were when you made the appointment to see me. Where on the scale would you like to be at the end of this therapy? What will be different in your life then? Where are you on that scale today? How is it not lower than it is? What will one point higher look like? How will you/others know you are one point higher? What will you be doing differently? Who or what can help you to reach a higher point?"

In the next chapter, we will see how in follow-up sessions the focus is on small steps forward. Taking small steps encompasses a low threshold and low risk, greater chances of success, and often a snowball effect, leading to bigger changes.

7

Working on Progress

Introduction

In follow-up sessions, clients and therapists explore what has improved. The focus is on small steps forward. When problems are large and overwhelming, taking small steps is even more powerful than big leaps. Small steps ("baby steps") have the following advantages: a low threshold, low risk, greater chances of successes, and a possible snowball effect, enabling bigger changes.

Progress can also be made through inviting clients to rewrite their negative stories into more helpful and compassionate ones or to use positive imagery (see Volume 2: Depression and Volume 3: Trauma). Homework suggestions, intended to direct clients' attention to those aspects of their situation that are most useful in reaching their goal, may be added to enhance further progress.

Follow-Up Sessions

"What is better (since we last met)?" is an invaluable opening in follow-up sessions, even if clients have been attending for a long time. Ask for a detailed description of what is better, give compliments, and emphasize the clients' input. At the end of the session, ask clients whether they think another session would be useful, and if so, when they want to return. In fact, in many cases clients think it isn't necessary to return, or they schedule an appointment further into the future than is typical in other forms of psychotherapy.

According to De Shazer (1994), the goal of follow-up sessions is to ask questions about the time between sessions in such a way that clients can discern some progress. If one looks carefully, one can (virtually) always find improvements. Another aim is to see whether clients think that what the therapist and client did in the previous session has been useful and has given them the sense that things are better. Follow-up sessions also serve to help clients find out what they are doing or what has happened that has led to improvements, so that they will know what to do more of. Other aims are to help clients work out whether things are going well enough that further sessions are not necessary, and to ensure that therapists and clients do not do more of what doesn't work and seek a new approach instead.

There is no limit to the number of sessions in SFBT. The sessions are ended when clients achieve their goal (to a sufficient degree). After the second session, the time interval between sessions usually increases. One week between the first and the second session is generally a good amount of time (but it can be more or less if clients so wish). Traditional psychotherapy usually schedules one or more sessions regularly every week or every two weeks. In SFBT, each session is scheduled according to:

- The time needed for the performance of a homework assignment
- The promotion of confidence in the solutions
- The promotion of independence from therapy
- The client's responsibility for therapy

Some homework suggestions take more time to do or to bring about a meaningful difference for clients. Spacing out the sessions enables clients to have a longer perspective on their construction of solutions and to put setbacks in perspective. The spacing of sessions over longer periods of time, from two weeks to three to six, also promotes confidence, since some clients think that changing is dependent on therapy and that their therapists are responsible for the change. The spacing of sessions is determined by clients and not by therapists; the therapist asks, "Do you think it is useful to schedule another session, and if so, when would you like to return?"

Assessing Progress

Change is happening all the time; the role of therapists is to find useful change and amplify it. How do therapists and clients know they are moving in the right direction? Monitoring progress is essential and improves the chances of success (Duncan, 2005, p. 183). "You don't really need the perfect approach as much as you need to know whether your plan is working—and if it is not, how to quickly adjust your strategy to maximize the possibility of improvement." Absence of early improvement decreases the chances of achieving what clients want to achieve. When no improvement occurs by the third session, progress isn't likely to occur over the entire course of treatment. Moreover, people who didn't indicate that therapy was helping by the sixth session were likely to receive no benefit, despite the length of therapy. The diagnosis and the type of therapy were not as important in predicting success as knowing whether the treatment was actually working. Clients whose therapists got feedback about the lack of progress were, at the conclusion of therapy, better off than 65% of those whose therapists didn't receive this information. Clients whose therapists had access to progress information were less likely to get worse with treatment and were twice as likely to achieve a clinically significant change.

The opening question "What is better?" suggests that some progress has been made and that one only needs to pay attention to what is better. This question is different from "Is anything better?" or "What went well" or "How are you doing?" or "How have things been since our last session?" Clients usually react to this question with surprise. Sometimes clients initially respond by saying "Nothing," because that is what they experience from their point of view; they have not given any thought to anything better. In that case, therapists ask questions about the recent past and look for times when the problem was absent or less of a problem.

Working on the assumption that one can always find exceptions if one looks for them, SF therapists ask questions not about *whether* there are exceptions but about *when* there are /were exceptions. Alternatives to "What is better?" are "What is different?" or "What have you been pleased to notice?" Therapists may also ask the four basic SF questions presented in Chapter 2.

De Jong and Berg (2002) developed the acronym *EARS* to distinguish the activities in follow-up sessions. *E* stands for *eliciting* (drawing out stories about progress and exceptions). *A* stands for *amplifying.* Clients are invited to describe the differences between the moment when the exception took place and problematic moments. Therapists and clients examine how the exception took place, especially what role the client played in it. *R* stands for *reinforcing.* Therapists reinforce the successes and factors that have led to the exceptions through the exploration of these exceptions and by complimenting clients. *S* stands for *start again*: "What else is better?"

Clients may provide *four different response patterns* to "What is better?" How well clients are doing and whether the homework suits them determines whether therapists should continue on the same path or should do something else. Therapists should always tailor their questions and homework suggestions to the alliance with each client (see Chapter 4). It is important to keep in mind that clients want their problem solved, however pessimistic or skeptical they may be. For that reason, it is important to listen closely and to examine *how* clients want to change. In follow-up sessions, it is vital to optimize the alliance and to retain progress already made and build on it. In addition, therapists need to verify whether the homework has been useful, and any possible regression must be caught. The four responses are: (1) Things are better, (2) We disagree (if is more than one client), (3) Things are the same, and (4) Things are worse. The good news is that for all four responses, SF strategies are available (Bannink, 2010a, 2010c, 2014a, 2014b).

CASE 8. NOTHING IS BETTER

"Nothing is better" is the client's answer to the question about progress. The therapist invites the client to first tell her more about the worst moment in the past week. After acknowledging this difficult moment, the therapist switches to questions about exceptions: "So the other moments must have been somewhat better. Please tell me more about those moments. What was better about these moments, and what exactly did you do to make these moments happen?"

STORY 13. A POSITIVE DIFFERENCE

A boy was picking something up and throwing it into the ocean. A man approached him and asked, "What are you doing?" The boy replied, "I am saving the starfish that have been stranded on the beach. The tide is going out, and if I don't throw them back, they will die." The man noticed that there were miles and miles of beach and thousands of starfish. He looked at the beach again and then at the boy and said, "Well, you won't make much of a difference, will you?"

The little boy picked up another starfish, and threw it back into the sea. Then, looking up, he smiled and said, "I made a difference for that one!"

In changing repetitive patterns, O'Hanlon (1999) states that many psychotherapists think it takes years to make a significant change, especially with serious, long-standing problems, but the SF approach shows that people can make changes rapidly. SFBT focuses on the present and the future and encourages clients to take action and change their points of view. The past is important in the sense that it has influenced us and has brought us to where we are today, but letting it determine our future is a mistake. Instead, SFBT acknowledges the past and then gets on with changing things. O'Hanlon offers three keys for clients to break repetitive problem patterns.

Key 1: *Change the doing of the problem.* To solve a problem or change things that are not going well, change any part you can of your regularly repeated actions in the situation: Do something different. For example, when you are feeling anxious, instead of staying in, go outside and talk with somebody.

Key 2: *Use paradox.* Go with the problem or try to make it worse (more intense or more frequent) or try to deliberately make the problem happen. Stop trying to fix the problem or make the situation better. This works best for emotional or bodily problems like insomnia, anxiety, phobias, panic, and sexual problems. For example, when you are feeling anxious, instead of avoiding the situation, use a mindfulness exercise and watch anxiety come and go.

Key 3: *Link new actions to the problem pattern.* Find something you can do every time you have the problem—something that is good for you. Find something that you think you should do, but usually avoid or put off. Every time you feel the urge to "do" the problem, do the avoided action first. If you are not able to do that, do the avoided action for the same amount of time as the problem action, after the problem is over. Make the problem an ordeal by linking it to something unpleasant. Add something new, usually burdensome, to the situation, every time the problem occurs. For example, when you have had a few drinks too many, do extra fitness exercises the next day.

The suggestion to do something different can also be used if clients complain about another person and claim to have tried everything. Solutions involve doing something that is different from what didn't work before (see Story 14).

STORY 14. DO SOMETHING DIFFERENT

A 10-year-old boy was apprehended for prowling around his school. He had broken in to get his homework, which he had forgotten; however, he refused to answer the policeman's questions. Once the policeman had tried everything to get him to talk, he threatened to hold his own breath until the boy explained why he had broken into the school. This proved too much for the boy. He revealed that he had broken in to retrieve his homework so as not to get a failing grade (De Shazer, 1991).

Clients should become *amygdala whisperers.* We want our clients to be able to be conscious of their amygdala activation and say, "Don't worry; everything will be fine." Amygdala activation takes place if constitutional features, traumatic experiences, or negative attachments have produced maladaptive emotion regulation, restricting people in their ability to achieve emotional resilience and behavioral flexibility. Addressing the neocortex can override these responses and bring the deeper structures of the amygdala into a more tolerable level of arousal. This can be done by a number of "self-talk" strategies in which imagery or internal dialogue is activated. Over time and with continued practice, the frequency and intensity of these responses can be significantly decreased, and the speed of recovery can be enhanced (see Case 9).

CASE 9. FEAR OF DOGS

Siegel (1999) describes a client with a fear of dogs after having been mauled by one; he had lost part of his left ear and sustained deep wounds to his arms and chest. Teaching him about the nature of the fear response and the neural circuits underlying it was relieving for him, and relaxation techniques and guided imagery with exposure to self-generated images of dogs were provided. Nevertheless, he still had a startle response to dogs, so a *cognitive override strategy* was used. He learned to acknowledge the relevance of his amygdala's response to the present dog and the past trauma (the initial arousal mechanism). He would say to himself, "I know that you (the amygdala) are trying to protect me, and that you think this is a dangerous thing" (the specific appraisal stage). What he would say next was what eventually allowed him to buy his children a dog: "I don't need to see this sense of panic as something to fear or get agitated about." He would then imagine his amygdala sighing with relief, having discharged its duties to warn, and the sense of doom would dissipate. After several weeks of performing these internal override discussions, he felt ready to proceed with the purchase of the pet. Six months later, he and his family were doing well with the new addition to their household.

Close to 50% of clients diagnosed with an anxiety disorder also meet the criteria for a depressive disorder (see Chapter 1). *Gratitude* counterbalances depression, because it changes clients' focus from what is wrong to what is right in the world and in their lives. The concept of gratitude involves more than an interpersonal appreciation of other people's aid. It is part of a wider life orientation toward noticing and appreciating the positive. This life orientation is distinct from other emotions such as optimism, hope, and trust.

While these may involve life orientations, these would not characteristically be geared toward noticing and appreciating the positive in life. For example, optimism represents a life orientation toward positive expectations of future outcomes. Hope incorporates this focus, as well as the tendency to see the ways through which these positive outcomes may be reached.

Gratitude is strongly related to well-being (Wood, Froh, & Geraghty, 2010). Interventions to clinically increase gratitude are promising due to strong explanatory power in understanding well-being and the potential of improving well-being through fostering gratitude with simple exercises (see Volume 2: Depression).

Research on gratitude (Seligman, 2002) shows that:

- Expressing gratitude has a short-time positive effect (several weeks) on happiness levels (up to a 25% increase). Those who are typically or habitually grateful are happier than those who aren't habitually grateful.
- People who note weekly the things they are grateful for increase their happiness levels 25% over people who note their complaints or are just asked to note any events during the week.
- People who scored as severely depressed were instructed to recall and write down three good things that happened each day for 15 days. Clients were invited to set aside 10 minutes every night and write down three things that went well that day and why they went well. Ninety-four % of them went from severely depressed to between mildly to moderately depressed during that time.

STORY 15. SAIL AWAY FROM THE SAFE HARBOR

Mark Twain stated, "Twenty years from now, you will be more disappointed by the things that you didn't do than by the ones you did do. So throw off the bowlines. Sail away from the safe harbor. Catch the trade winds in your sails. Explore. Dream. Discover" (as quoted in Burns, Duncan, & Ward, 2001).

EXERCISE 19. SAFE PLACE

Invite clients to visualize a *safe place*. This is an excellent way to reduce stress and anxiety. Ask them to select a place they have been at any time in their life or a place they make up in fantasy that evokes a sense of peacefulness, calm, serenity, safety, and security. Examples are their own bed, a fantasy island where nobody can come unless invited, or a vault in a bank.

Ask them to take a couple of minutes per day to connect as closely as they can with their safe place. Ask them to think of all the details they like about it and how it makes them feel. Clients may do this exercise with their eyes open or closed, and may disclose what their safe place is or keep it to themselves.

EXERCISE 20. RELAXATION EXERCISE

Invite clients to take their mind off stress and replace it with an image that evokes a sense of calm. The more realistic the daydream in terms of colors, sights, sounds, and touch, the more relaxation they will experience. Ask clients to visualize a peaceful situation or *dreamscape*. This could be a favorite vacation spot, a fantasy island, a penthouse in New York City, or something touchable, like the feel of a favorite sweater or furry animal.

EXERCISE 21. LOVING-KINDNESS MEDITATION

Invite clients to find a place where they can sit comfortably without being disturbed. Ask them to rest their hands lightly on their lap, palms up, to close their eyes and take a few deep breaths. Say, "Just let it be, and just continue to observe your breath. The goal in attending to your breath is to practice being present, here and now. There is no need to suppress your thoughts; just let them be and become aware of them as they come and fade away again."

Mindfulness exercises are used to cultivate *loving-kindness*. Invite clients to first reflect on a person (or animal) for whom they feel warm and compassionate feelings. Once these feelings take hold, creating positivity in them, ask them to gently let go of the image and simply hold the feeling. Then ask them to extend that feeling to themselves, cherishing themselves as deeply and purely as they would cherish their own newborn child. Next, ask them to radiate their warm and compassionate feelings to others, first to someone they know well, then gradually to other friends and family members, and then to all people with whom they are connected, even remotely. Ultimately, ask them to extend their feelings of love and kindness to all people and creatures of the earth: "May they all be happy" (Fredrickson, 2009).

Compassionate people go easy on themselves. More details about *self-compassion*, SF questions to enhance self-compassion, and exercises are described in Volume 2: Depression and Volume 3: Trauma.

CASE 10. A PILLOW, A PANTHER, AND AN ANGEL

In the Netherlands, there is a rhyme about a store where you can buy anything you want (Winkel van Sinkel). You may buy a pound of courage, a lion that protects you against danger, or a balance to weigh every request first before you say yes or no. Invite clients to enter this store, have a look around, and choose one or more things that may help them to reach their goal. Everything is free and they may return and change any item if it doesn't suit them. What is special about this store is that clients may also leave behind anything they don't need anymore, but someone else may find useful, such as a bag with perfectionism. Invite clients to use their new items and observe how these items help them move forward.

The client feels very anxious when doing exams. Because this fear is holding back her career, she wants to get some help. The therapist proposes that she imagines she visits the Winkel van Sinkel. After she has looked around a bit, she chooses three items: a beautiful white embroidered pillow on which she can lay her weary head; a black panther who will enter the scary exam forest first; and a little angel sitting on her right shoulder that compliments her (instead of the little devil sitting on her left shoulder that always criticizes her). She chooses not to leave anything behind in the store. At home she practices with the pillow, panther, and angel by rehearsing how she will do her exams. Later on, she brings her three imaginary items with her to the exams and succeeds in passing them.

EXERCISE 22. DESIGN YOURSELF A BEAUTIFUL DAY

Invite clients to *design themselves a beautiful day*. Ask them to plan the enjoyable things they will be doing that day, where they will be, and with whom. Ask them to design the beautiful day or a beautiful half day in a way that uses their strengths and talents. If, for example, one of their main strengths is curiosity and love of learning, their day might include a trip to a museum or reading a book. When the beautiful day arrives, ask them to employ their savoring and mindfulness skills to enhance these pleasures. A variation is *setting a strengths date* for couples, in which both partners use their strengths during the date.

Homework Suggestions

Many forms of psychotherapy consider homework to be important. However, De Shazer (1985) stated that he could get as much information when clients didn't perform homework. He found that accepting nonperformance as a message about the clients' way of doing things (rather than as a sign of resistance; see Chapter 5) allowed him to develop a cooperative relationship with clients that might not include homework. This was a shock to him, because he had assumed that homework was necessary to achieve behavioral change.

Nevertheless, at the end of each session, therapists may offer clients homework suggestions, intended to direct their attention to those aspects of their experiences and situations that are most useful in reaching their goals.

Clients in a *customer-relationship* may get observation and behavior suggestions (suggestions to actually do something different). Therapy with these clients is often the "icing on the cake" and gives some much needed positive reinforcement to therapists that they are competent.

In a *visitor-relationship*, no suggestions are given. After all, the problem has not yet been defined, nor is there any talk of a goal or related exceptions. Therapists go along with their clients' worldview, extend acknowledgment, and compliment them on their strengths and resources and for coming to the therapist's office. They propose another appointment to continue to find out with clients what would be the best thing for them to do.

In a *complainant-relationship*, only observational suggestions are given. To clients who cannot name exceptions or a goal, therapists may give one of the following suggestions:

- "Pay attention to what happens in your life that gives you the idea that the problem can be solved.";
- "Reflect on what you would like to accomplish with these sessions."
- "Pay attention to what is going well and should stay the same" or "Pay attention to what happens in your life that you would like to continue to happen."
- "Observe the positive moments in your life."
- "Pay attention to the times when things are better."
- If scaling questions are used: "Observe when you are one point higher on the scale and what you and/or (significant) others are doing differently then."
- "Pay attention to what gives you hope that the problem can be solved."

The use of observation suggestions implies that exceptions may occur again and can contribute to clients' feeling more hopeful. These suggestions also indicate that useful information can be found within the clients' own realm of experience.

When clients are hesitant about change, therapists should suggest that they *observe* rather than *do* something. The thought of doing something might seem too big a step; an observational task might not seem as threatening. Since clients don't have the pressure to do anything different, they might be more likely to observe what they are already doing. By doing this, they will probably find more exceptions. If clients don't (yet) have any ideas about which step forward they might take, *observation suggestions about exceptions* are useful:

- "Observe when things are just a little bit better and what you did to make that happen."
- "Observe situations when the problem is there to a lesser extent, even just a little bit."
- "Observe situations where the problem is present and you succeed in coping a bit better with it."

De Shazer (1988) sometimes adds an element of *prediction*. If there are exceptions, a prediction task suggests that they will occur again, maybe even sooner than clients imagine. If clients predict a better day, they will be more inclined to look for signs of confirmation (*positive self-fulfilling prophecy*). Clients in a complainant-relationship, who can describe spontaneous exceptions, may receive such a prediction task (see Exercise 23).

EXERCISE 23. PREDICTION SUGGESTION

Invite clients to:

- Predict what tomorrow will be like, find an explanation for why the day turned out the way it did tomorrow evening, and then make a new prediction for the following day
- Find out what contributed to the prediction's coming true or not coming true

CASE 11. FIRST SESSION FORMULA TASK

At the end of the first session, therapists may give clients the *first session formula task*: "Between now and the next time we meet, I would like you to observe what happens in your life that you want to continue to happen." This intervention defines therapy as dealing with the present and the future rather than the past. The therapist expects something worthwhile to happen, and this is often the opposite of what clients expect to happen. The suggestion lets clients know that the therapist is confident that change will occur. This is an easy task for clients to cooperate with, since it doesn't call for anything different; only observations are required. This is something clients will do anyway, and this suggestion directs the focus of their observations.

Clients who say that things are worse often have a long history of failure or have contended with big problems for years. If therapists are too optimistic, they will be unable to help them. These clients often need a lot of space to tell the story of the problem, including any (negative) experiences with previous therapists. SF questions to invite *clients who report that things are worse* to think about are:

- ■ "How do I manage to go on under these circumstances?"
- ■ "How come I haven't given up by now?"
- ■ "How come things aren't worse than they are?"
- ■ "What is the smallest thing I could do to make a minimal difference?"
- ■ "What can others do for me?"
- ■ "What can I remember about what used to help that I could try again now?"
- ■ "What would most help me climb back into the saddle and face these difficulties?"

More strategies for working with pessimistic clients are described in Volume 2: Depression. Suggestions to predict the next crisis and how to cope with suicidal feelings are described in Chapter 4.

It is useful to put pessimistic clients in an expert position and ask them, as *consultants*, what their treatment should look like. SF questions for *expert clients* are:

- "What did therapists you worked with previously miss?"
- "Of all the things that these therapists did, what did you find most disagreeable?"
- "How can I be of greater assistance?"
- "What qualities would your ideal therapist have, and what would he or she do?"
- "What questions would your ideal therapist ask you, and what, in your opinion, would be the best course for him or her to follow?"
- "If I worked with other clients who were in the same boat as you, what advice would you give me that would allow me to help them?"
- "What question can you think of that would allow me to help you the most?"

CASE 12. PRETEND TO FEEL DIFFERENT

The client was given the following homework suggestion. On the odd-numbered days of the week, he was to pretend to feel different and see what happened. He was told he might not always feel that way; however, there might be some potential to act and think differently. He was invited to pretend to feel different on odd-numbered days and on the even-numbered days just to do as he normally would. During follow-up sessions, the therapist asked him what differences he noticed.

An alternative is to invite clients to pretend that the miracle has happened, when the *miracle question* (see Chapter 5) has been asked. Clients are invited to choose one day or half day of the week and pretend the miracle has happened and notice the differences in their mood and behavior and how others react differently. Yet another possibility is to ask partners in couples therapy or a family to all pretend one day a week that their miracle has happened and not tell the others which day it is, and then each person has to guess when the other(s) were pretending it was their miracle (half) day.

EXERCISE 24. WORST CASE SCENARIO

If very pessimistic clients are expecting a visit or planning a holiday they are dreading, ask them to pretend they are the director of a movie in which their family members are playing their usual parts (the ones that drive them or others crazy) and that their job is to get them to deliver their lines or do their usual behaviors to perfection.

Or invite them to imagine some *worst case scenarios* before the visit/holiday takes place and compare what actually happens to those scenarios to see if they even come close (most of the times they don't).

SF questions in this chapter are:

77. "What is better (since we last met)?" or "What is different?" or "What have you been pleased to notice?" "What else is better?"
78. "Do you think it is useful to schedule another session?" If so, "When would you like to return?"
79. "So the other moments must have been somewhat better. Please tell me more about those moments. What was better about these moments, and what exactly did you do to make these moments happen?"
80. "What did therapists you worked with previously miss? Of all the things that these therapists did, what did you find most disagreeable? How can I be of greater assistance?"
81. "What qualities would your ideal therapist have, and what would he or she do? What questions would your ideal therapist ask you, and what, in your opinion, would be the best course for them to follow?"
82. "If I worked with other clients who were in the same boat as you, what advice would you give me that would allow me to help them?"

In the next chapter, we will see how SFBT ensures that clients are in the driver's seat. They decide when to conclude therapy. Behavior maintenance replaces the term *relapse prevention*, and suggestions are given on how to deal with impasses and failures. Right at the start of therapy, clients may be invited to think, already, about how to celebrate successes, the conclusion of therapy, or victory over anxiety.

8

Concluding Therapy

Introduction

Discussing the preferred future from the beginning of therapy generates optimism and hope. Clients indicate whether they think another session is useful and when to end therapy. Instead of relapse prevention, SFBT pays attention to the progress made and how to maintain these positive changes. Also, four pathways to impasse and failure are described. Right at the start of therapy, clients are invited to think about how to celebrate successes, the concluding of therapy, or their victory over anxiety.

Concluding Therapy

If therapists accept clients' statement of the problem at the start of treatment, by the same logic, therapists should accept the clients' declaration that they have sufficiently improved as a reason to end treatment (De Shazer, 1991). Each session is viewed as potentially the last, and sometimes just one session may be enough.

Contrary to traditional psychotherapies, discussion around ending therapy occurs as soon as therapy starts, as is evident from the questions about goal formulation: "What would indicate to you that you're doing well enough that you no longer have to come here?" In this way, therapists wish to elicit is a description of what clients consider a successful result, in positive, concrete, and measurable terms. A detailed description of the preferred future is key: "What will you be doing differently that tells me that that's the situation you prefer?" The moment when the sessions can be concluded may also be revealed by means of scaling questions: "What point do you/important others/the referrer think you should be at on a scale of 10 to 0 in order not to have to come to therapy anymore?" Sometimes treatment can be concluded at a rather low point on the scale, because clients have gained enough hope, confidence, and motivation that they can move toward the point they would like to end up at without therapy.

Behavior Maintenance

Relapse prevention is a standard intervention toward the end of therapy, but what are therapists actually suggesting or predicting when they talk about relapse? Of course, maintaining hard-won changes isn't easy, and clients have to work hard and show determination to do so. Instead of talking about relapses and how to prevent them, it is preferable to talk about the progress made and how to maintain these positive changes. In this vein, relapse prevention becomes behavior maintenance.

Focusing on what clients (and others) have done to help recovery or prevention in past experiences is useful. Therapists may map out a *recovery plan*—especially with clients who have severe mental problems, like major depression or suicidal thoughts. This can usually be derived from asking about what happened as the client regains equilibrium after a previous crisis or hospitalization (see Chapter 4).

EXERCISE 25. FIFTY WAYS TO MAINTAIN POSITIVE CHANGE

Do you remember the song "Fifty Ways to Leave Your Lover" by Paul Simon? Making lists is often a fun and challenging task for clients:

- Think of 50 good reasons to maintain the positive changes you made.
- Think of 50 ways to maintain these positive changes.
- Think of 50 positive consequences (for yourself/important others) of maintaining these positive changes.

SF questions for *behavior maintenance* are:
- "How do/did you manage to get back on the right track?"
- "How do/did you find the courage to get back on the right track and not throw in the towel?"

- "How do you know that you have the strength and courage to get back on the right track?"
- "What other qualities do you have that you can you use to help yourself do that?"
- "What can you do to ensure that you maintain these positive results?"
- "On a scale of 10 to 0, where 10 equals great confidence and 0 equals no confidence at all, how much confidence do you have now?" (and follow-up scaling questions).
- "On a scale of 10 to 0, where 10 equals being very motivated and 0 equals being not motivated at all, how motivated are you to maintain these positive changes?"
- "What can you remember and use from these sessions if a time comes when things are not going as well as they are now?"

CASE 13. HOW DID YOU SUCCEED
IN STAYING AWAY THAT LONG?

The client has overcome a previous depressive episode with the help of SFBT and medication. One year later she requests another appointment because she is feeling depressed again. When she starts talking about what is wrong, the therapist asks her permission to pose a somewhat strange question: "How did you succeed in staying away that long?" The client reacts surprised and describes how, apart from the previous two weeks, last year actually has been a good one: She has been able to work, she and her husband made a trip to Asia, and she has been singing in the choir again. By telling how well she has been doing, she brightens up and is already feeling somewhat better.

The therapist compliments her on making such a timely appointment and at the end of the session asks her whether she thinks another session would be useful. The client thinks one session is enough and promises to return in case of deterioration. One year later she emails that she is doing fine.

Impasse and Failure

The average treated client is better off than about 80% of the untreated sample (Duncan, Miller, Wampold, & Hubble, 2010). But dropouts are a significant problem, and although many clients profit from therapy, many don't. Sometimes clients come back and say that things are worse, or nothing has changed. This may be discouraging for therapists and clients, especially when everybody has worked hard.

Clients may feel embarrassed or ashamed at having to report failure or setbacks. The importance of *saving face* is discussed below. Moreover, even very effective clinicians seem to be poor at identifying deteriorating clients. Hannan et al. (2005) found that although therapists knew the purpose of their study, were familiar with the outcome measures, and were informed that the base rate was likely to be 8%, they accurately predicted deterioration in only 1 out of 40 clients!

Duncan, Hubble, and Miller (1997) describe four pathways to impossibility.

The first pathway arises in the *anticipation of impossibility*. Therapists' expectation of impossibility will probably distort new information to conform to their expectations. The famous experiment of Rosenhan and his colleagues (Rosenhan, 1973) is described in Story 16.

The second pathway to impossibility is *therapists' traditions or conventions*. Therapists are often eager to corroborate their theory with each client, and their theory is often overapplied. Remember the story of the man who bought a hammer and then found that everything needed to be nailed?

Clients have their own theories about their lives and problems. When their points of view are ignored or dismissed by the therapist's theory, noncompliance or resistance is a predictable outcome. To therapists, clients begin to look, feel, and act in impossible ways; to clients, therapists come across as uncaring or disinterested. The therapy changes from a helping relationship to a clash of cultures with no winners.

The third pathway to impossibility is *persisting in an approach that isn't working*. Watzlawick, Weakland, and Fisch (1974) reasoned that unmanageable problems, those that are often called "chronic," couldn't be sufficiently explained on the basis of innate characteristics of the clients. Rather, they concluded that the unyielding or impossible nature of a problem arises in the very efforts to solve it. For a difficulty to turn into a problem, only two conditions need to be fulfilled: First, the difficulty is mishandled; the attempted solutions don't work. Second, when the difficulty proves refractory, more of the same ineffective solutions are applied and the original difficulties deteriorate. Over time, a vicious downward spiral ensues, with the original difficulty growing into an impasse, immense in size and importance.

Therapists who do more of the same are sometimes convinced that persistence will eventually win the day, even when all evidence suggests that their strategy is ineffectual. All theoretical models and strategies are limited and will generate their share of impossibility when repetitively applied. Wampold (2001) found that when there is no improvement after the third session, chances are 75% that therapy with fail. This percentage is 90% when no improvement is found after the sixth session. Lambert and Ogles (2004) found that treatment should be brief when little or no progress is made in the early sessions; then it should be as short in duration as possible. Therapy should not be used for the purpose of just sustaining or maintaining clients. However, as long as clients are making documentable progress and are interested in continuing, treatment should be continued.

Piper and his colleagues (1999) found that dropouts could be predicted by treatment process variables, not by client variables. In other words, only what happened in the sessions predicted whether the client failed to return, not who the client was and what the client brought to the process.

The fourth and last pathway to impossibility is created when therapists *neglect clients' motivation*. There is no such individual as an unmotivated client. Clients may not share the ideas and goal of their therapists, but they hold strong motivations of their own. An unproductive therapy can come about by mistaking or overlooking what clients want to accomplish, misapprehending their readiness for change, or pursuing a personal motivation. Research shows that the critical process-outcome in psychotherapy is the quality of the client's participation in a positive *alliance* (see Chapter 4). The motivation of clients for not only sitting in the therapist's office, but also for achieving their goal, has to be understood, respected, and actively incorporated into therapy. To do less or to impose agendas motivated by theoretical prerogatives, personal bias, and perhaps a sense of what would be good for clients invites impossibility.

SF questions and tips for therapists for *solving impasses* are:

- "Does the client want to change (e.g., do I have a customer-relationship with this client)?"
- "What is the client's goal?"
- "Does the client have a goal and not a wish? Is the goal well-defined and within the control of the client?"
- "Am I and the client looking for too much too fast?" If so, look for a smaller change.
- "Does the client not do the homework?" Provide some feedback to think about rather than an action-oriented task.
- "If I have gone through all the above steps, is there anything I need to do differently?" Sometimes we are too close to the trees to see the forest and may not recognize a nonproductive pattern between the client and us. A team or consultant may be helpful to provide a more detached frame of reference.

STORY 16. THE ROSENHAN EXPERIMENT

Rosenhan (1973) recruited and trained a group of normal colleagues to obtain psychiatric hospitalization. To gain admission, they falsified a single psychotic symptom (hearing voices). The clinicians diagnosed the pretend patients as mentally ill and admitted them for stays ranging from 7 to 52 days. During their hospitalizations, the pseudo-patients showed no signs of psychosis, yet the original diagnosis remained in place. Rosenhan also demonstrated how the clinician's initial expectations came to serve as confirmatory biases. In one instance, staff took truthful historical information provided by a pseudo-patient and made it conform to prevailing theoretical notions about schizophrenia.

CASE 14. CLIENT WORSENING

Is it to be expected that clients will get worse before they get better? Of course not! Considerable clinical lore has built up around the idea that deterioration of the client's situation comes before the situation gets better. This is rarely the road to recovery and is an indicator that portends a final negative outcome. This idea also allows therapists to ignore, to some degree, client worsening (Lambert & Ogles, 2004).

If a setback occurs, therapists should normalize it: Progress often means taking three steps forward and one or two steps back (and it would be a shame to give up even a single step). Therapists may also give a positive slant to the setback; after all, a setback offers an opportunity to practice getting back on one's feet. If you fall on your face, at least you are heading in the right direction (O'Hanlon, 2000).

It is often not necessary to dwell on the cause of the relapse and its consequences. Therapists would do well to offer acknowledgement by showing that they understand how frustrating the relapse is to clients. Following this, it is important to explore how clients have managed on previous occasions to get back on the right track.

Clients (or their therapists) can also deal with relapse in a lighter, more playful manner: "What would it take for me to go back to square one as quickly as possible?" This immediately indicates what the wrong approach is and often lends the conversation a lighthearted tenor.

Berg and Steiner (2003) also invite therapists to ask themselves some questions if there is no progress (see Volume 2: Depression and Volume 3: Trauma). Other SF questions to *create new openings* are:

- "What would be the best question I could ask you right now?"
- "If there was a last question you would like me to ask, what would it be?"

When clients feel overwhelmed and stuck, *saving face* is important. Clients are apt to experience their problems as impossible; seeking help offers the prospect of something better. Simultaneously, seeking help may also signify their failure to solve the problem on their own. Needing therapy can represent just one more unpleasant reminder of how badly they have managed their difficulties. If therapists suggest that the client's point of view is wrong, the alliance will deteriorate. What some colleagues call *resistance* may reflect the client's attempt to salvage a portion of self-respect. Some cases become impossible because the treatment allows clients no way of saving face or upholding dignity. This is what Erickson had in mind when he suggested that the art of therapy revolves around helping clients *to bow out of their symptoms gracefully*. He recognized that clients simultaneously hold a desire to change and a natural tendency to protect themselves if change compromises personal dignity.

CASE 15. DEADLOCK

The client suffering from a panic disorder says, "I don't think this therapy will be helpful; the former therapy was no success either. I made a plan to change things in my life, but I have been too afraid to actually do most of the experiments." The (overoptimistic) therapist ignores this remark and starts using a therapeutic protocol with exposure exercises, and before long therapy reaches an impasse.

The therapist would have done better to validate the client's doubts by acknowledging them and by asking scaling questions with respect to confidence, hope, and motivation: "Supposing you had a bit more hope that this therapy will be beneficial, what difference would that make?" and "Where, despite your previous negative experiences, did you find the courage to reenter therapy?"

Celebrating Success

At the start of therapy, therapists may ask already, "How will you celebrate your success when you have reached your goal?" or "How will you celebrate your victory over Anxiety/Panic/Worry?" Children and families in particular find this an enjoyable way to start. A celebration gives clients closure on the goal they have been working toward. It provides encouragement to continue and makes every success even more worthwhile. The celebration doesn't have to be a big deal; it can be something clients do alone or share with others. It just has to make them feel good and help them enjoy their accomplishment. Suggestions for celebrations are described in Volume 2: Depression.

SF questions in this chapter are:

83. "What would indicate to you that you're doing well enough that you no longer have to come here?" or "What will you be doing differently that tells me that that's the situation you prefer?"

84. "What point do you/important others/the referrer think you should be at on a scale of 10 to 0 in order not to have to come to therapy anymore?"

85. "How do/did you manage to get back on the right track?" or "How did you find the courage to get back on the right track and not throw in the towel?" or "How do you know that you will have the strength and courage to get back on the right track?" "What other qualities do you have that you can use to help yourself do that?"

86. "What can you do to ensure that you maintain these positive results? On a scale of 10 to 0, where 10 equals great confidence and 0 equals no confidence at all, how much confidence do you have that you can maintain these results? On a scale of 10 to 0, where 10 equals being very motivated and 0 equals not being motivated at all, how motivated are you to maintain these positive changes?"

87. "What can you remember and use from these sessions if a time comes when things are not going as well as they are now?"

88. "How did you succeed in staying away as long as you did?"

89. "What would be the best question I could ask you now?" or "If there was a last question you would like me to ask, what would it be?"

90. "Supposing you had a bit more hope that this therapy will be beneficial, what difference would that make?" "Where, despite your previous negative experiences, did you find the courage to reenter therapy?"

91. "How will you celebrate your success when you have reached your goal?" or "How will you celebrate your victory over anxiety/panic/worry?"

In the next chapter, we will see how therapists improve their success by asking themselves reflective questions. Also, feedback from clients is essential for a successful outcome of therapy and for developing therapists' skills.

9

Reflection and Feedback

Introduction

Therapists should take the time to reflect on their contribution to the sessions so that they may continue to develop their skills. Furthermore, feedback from clients is essential and improves therapists' rate of success. Asking feedback invites clients to be full and equal partners in all aspects of therapy.

Reflecting on the Session

Research offers strong evidence that not all therapists perform equally well and that most therapists are poor judges of client deterioration. They are not good judges of their own performance either. Sapyta, Riemer, and Bickman (2005) asked clinicians of all types to rate their job performance from A+ to F. About 66% ranked themselves A or B. Not one therapist rated himself or herself as being below average! If you remember how the bell curve works, you know this isn't logically possible.

In the case of a successful treatment, and in the case of stagnation or failure, therapists should look back on what they did. Reflection can be done individually or with colleagues in the form of peer supervision (Bannink, 2014c). *Reflecting questions* for therapists are:

- "Supposing I was to conduct this session again, what would I do the same? What would I do differently?"
- "What would my client say I should do the same and/or differently?"
- "What difference would that make for him or her? What difference would that make for me?"
- "Supposing I conducted sessions in the future with clients with comparable problems, which interventions would I use again and which wouldn't I?"
- "What positive aspects of this treatment stand out?"
- "What does my client want to achieve in meeting with me?"
- "How satisfied do I think my client is with my performance (on a scale of 10 to 0)? What would he or she say about how I managed to get to that point? What would it look like for him or her if I were one point higher on the scale?"
- "How satisfied am I with my performance (on a scale of 10 to 0)? How did I manage to get to that point? What will one point higher look like? What difference will that make for the treatment?"
- "Which of my client's strengths and competencies and features did or can I compliment him or her on?"
- "What strengths and competencies can my client utilize with regard to the problem that brings him or her here?"

- "Which strengths and resources did I fail to capitalize on?"
- "Which resources from the environment can help my client?"
- "What do I see in my client that tells me that he or she can reach his or her goal?"

Clients' Feedback

Traditionally, the effectiveness of treatment has been left up to the judgment of the provider of this treatment. But proof of effectiveness emerges from clients' perception and experience as a full partner in the therapy process. Model and technique factors only represent 15% of outcome variance; they may or may not be useful in the client's circumstances. Therefore, therapists' theories should be deemphasized, and instead the focus should be on clients' theories. Exploring *their* ideas has several advantages:

- It puts clients center stage in the conversation
- It enlists clients' participation
- It ensures clients' positive experience of the professional
- It structures the conversation and directs the change process

It is the clients who matter: their resources, participation, evaluation of the alliance, and perceptions of the problem and solutions. The therapists' techniques are only helpful if clients see them as relevant and credible.

SF questions for asking *clients' feedback* are:

- "What feedback would you like to give me about today's session?
- "What has been most useful to you today?"
- "What have you gained from this session?"
- "What had you hoped to gain from this session that you haven't? How can we remedy that?"
- "What is the best or most valuable thing you've noticed about yourself today?"
- "What can you take from this session to reflect or work on in the coming period?"
- "What can you take from this session that can help you to . . . in the coming week?"
- "What can you take from this session that will enable you to tell me that things are better next time?"

Using clients' feedback to inform their therapists invites clients to be full and equal partners in all aspects of therapy. Giving clients the perspective of the driver's seat instead of the back of the bus enables them to gain confidence that a positive outcome is down the road (Miller, Duncan, & Hubble, 1997). Systematic assessment of the client's perceptions of progress and fit are important, so therapists can tailor therapy to the clients' needs and characteristics.

In traditional psychotherapy, progress is measured by a decrease in problems, and usually therapists decide when to stop therapy. "Too often the client is willing to accept the absence of the complaint as 'goal enough,' but the absence can never be proved and, therefore, success or failure cannot be known by either therapist or client" (De Shazer, 1991, p. 158).

Progress should, therefore, be measured by an increase in the desired situation. Apart from *scaling questions* about progress, clients may fill out the Session Rating Scale (SRS) at the end of each session. The SRS is a feedback instrument divided into the three areas that research has shown to be the qualities of change-producing relationships: (1) Alliance, (2) Goals and topics, and (3) Approach or method (allegiance). The SRS is an engagement instrument; it opens space for the clients' voice about the therapy. The scale is aimed at starting a conversation to improve therapy for the particular client. Dropout rates are lower if the SRS is used. Information about the SRS can be found at www.scottdmiller.com.

SF questions in this chapter are:

92. "What feedback would you like to give me about today's session?" or "What has been most useful to you today?" or "What have you gained from this session?"
93. "What had you hoped to gain from this session that you haven't? How can we remedy that?"
94. "What is the best or most valuable thing you've noticed about yourself today?"

95. "What can you take from this session to reflect or work on in the coming period?" or "What can you take from this session that can help you to . . . in the coming week?" or "What can you take from this session that will enable you to tell me that things are better next time?"

In the next chapter, we will focus on the well-being of clients; their partners, children, family members, and friends; and, last but not least, their therapists.

10

Focus on Well-Being

Introduction

Reducing distress by making miserable people less miserable is just one side of our job; building success by helping clients to flourish is the other side. Therefore, the focus on mental health should be added to the focus on mental illness. Clients' well-being also concerns their partners, children, family members, and friends. Paying attention to what they are doing right, future possibilities, past successes, and their strengths and resources, instead of what is wrong with them and their relationships, generates hope and helps them in building on what works and what might constitute progress. SFBT also promotes therapists' well-being and reduces the risk of burnout. Therapy may be fun and empowering (again) for its therapists.

Clients' Well-Being

Our capacity to change is connected to our ability to see things differently. These shifts in perceptions and definitions of reality, which are a part of solutions-building, occur in conversations about new and better lives and useful exceptions. SF therapists don't empower clients or construct alternative meanings for them; clients can only do that for themselves.

Psychotherapy should not be the place where clients just repair problems and weaknesses, but first and foremost it should be a place where clients build solutions and strengths. Therapy is aimed at increasing the well-being of our clients, thus ensuring that it will decrease psychopathology.

Anxiety and Relationships

Anxiety may give rise to impatience, suspicion, a lack of self-confidence, and a general sense of insecurity. Individuals suffering from an anxiety disorder may have an abnormal need for reassurance. Excessive worrying takes away a sense of well-being, often making the person irritable and snappy; short-tempered reactions may become more a norm than an exception. People suffering from anxiety are prone to seeking solace in the company of others, and this may not always be possible to accommodate. Furthermore, making these accommodations often actually exacerbates the anxiety. The demanding and clingy nature is bound to get on the partner's and children's nerves, prompting arguments and discord.

Having a partner or parent who struggles with anxiety can be difficult. Partners or children may find themselves in roles they don't want. They might get extra responsibilities and have to avoid certain places or activities that trigger their partner's or parent's anxiety. Partners or children of loved ones suffering from anxiety may find themselves angry, frustrated, sad, or disappointed that their dreams for what the relationship or family was going to be are limited by anxiety.

Anxiety and relationship issues may form a cause and effect cycle: Anxiety may lead to relationship issues, and the opposite is also true. The support of family members, children, and friends is necessary to recover from anxiety disorders. If symptoms are ignored and relationships bear the brunt of the disorder, then the person suffering from anxiety finds it even more difficult to cope with it.

Bannink (2008, 2009b, 2010b) offers tips for couples with problems and conflicts:

- If there is a struggle, suggest that both partners do something else, preferably something unexpected, and note the difference it makes.
- If there are arguments, ask partners what they do agree on.
- If there are arguments, ask partners if the situation could be worse. If so, how come it is not worse?
- If there is a conflict, ask partners what the other partner could do to encourage them to adopt a different attitude.
- If there is a conflict, ask partners what small signs they have detected that give them hope that the conflict can be resolved.
- If there are difficulties, invite partners to observe what the other person is doing to ameliorate the relationship (as a homework suggestion).

Difficulties in relationships are mostly attributed to poor communication. In response, therapists have focused their efforts on improving communication between partners, especially about problems and the expression of emotions. While effective communication has been linked to marital satisfaction in the research literature, Gordon, Baucom, Epstein, Burnett, and Rankin (1999) suggest a sometimes more effective alternative: *tolerance*. In particular, partners can be helped to become more tolerant (and probably more forgiving) when they adjust their expectations to the type of communication pattern they have. For example, avoidance of discussing problems and sharing emotions had less relation to marital satisfaction and happiness in couples that preferred more emotional and psychological space and less conjoint decision-making.

Also, many people suffering from an anxiety disorder don't have relationship problems. Relationships with others can offset feelings of being alone and help their self-esteem. Relationships can also give clients a way to help someone else. Helping others reduces feelings of failure or feeling cut off from others. Last, relationships are often a source of support when coping with stress and anxiety.

If *couples therapy* is needed, partners often come with a history of destructive and painful interactions, unable to work together to make the much-desired changes. It is important not to perpetuate this sense of failure, inadequacy, blame, and hopelessness by focusing on what the couple is doing wrong. Instead, a shift in focus to what they are doing right, future possibilities, past successes, and strengths and resources generates hope and helps couples in building on what works and what might constitute progress.

Ziegler and Hiller (2001) found that the best predictor of success is whether, early on, both partners begin to identify their individual and relationship strengths and become motivated to work together to bring about mutually desired changes. These changes take place if the couple turns into a *solution-building team*. As partners see themselves to be working as a solution-building team toward common goals, their hope, motivation, and effectiveness in making changes increases. And as they feel more hopeful about the future, they become more able to work collaboratively, both in therapy and in their everyday worlds.

Therapy starts by building a positive *alliance* with both partners. It is important to start building this alliance with the person who is more likely to be there involuntarily. Sometimes a partner is brought in for therapy because the other partner wants him or her to change.

SF questions about *strengths of the partner and the couple* are:

- "What is your partner good at?"
- "What do you appreciate in your partner?"
- "What aspects of your partner are you proud of?"
- "What is positive about your relationship?"
- "How did you meet each other? What attracted you in him/her?" (honeymoon talk)
- "Suppose you woke up tomorrow and your relationship had somehow been transformed to be exactly the way you envisioned it on your wedding day. What would you first notice as evidence of this change?"

The process of clients complimenting each other by describing each other's strengths generates hopefulness and goodwill, which usually makes the rest of the session proceed in a more positive tone. *Honeymoon talk* (Elliot, 2012) is also useful, because it changes the focus from problems to previous successes in the relationship.

Both partners are then invited to describe what they want different in their relationship. In this way clients, can move away from past problems and frustrations to something more productive and satisfying. "What would you like to see different in your relationship?" "What difference will it make if the other person changes in the direction you want him or her to change?" "What will be different between the two of you?" "What will you be doing differently then?"

In couples therapy, partners sometimes want the other person to change, which puts them in a *complainant-relationship* (see Chapter 4). Clients often speak of what they don't want or what they want to eliminate from their lives. In interactional situations, they often speak of what they want their partner *not* to do. He or she is still in the dark as to what the other does want to happen. Talking about what clients *do* want may open up the conversation in a more positive direction.

Therapists may ask about *exceptions*: "When is/was there a moment or a time when things between you are/were better, even just a little bit?" If clients cannot find exceptions, invite them to observe these moments in the time between sessions. Therapists may also use *scaling questions*:

- "Where on the scale from 10 to 0 would you like to end up (what will be a realistic goal), where 10 equals the best situation possible in your relationship and 0 equals the worst situation possible?"

- "At what point are you on the scale today (and how come it is not lower)?"
- "How will you know you are one point higher on the scale? What will be different between the two of you? What will you be doing differently?"
- "At what point on the scale do you think therapy may end?"

EXERCISE 26. HOMEWORK FOR A COUPLE OR FAMILY

This is another *homework suggestion* for a couple or family. "This week I want you to observe at least two things you see the other person(s) do to improve your relationship. Don't discuss this; just bring your observations to the next session." The purpose of this suggestion is for clients to start observing positive interactions instead of negative ones and to become more alert and willing to do positive things for the other person(s) now that they know this will be observed and reported.

EXERCISE 27. SUPPORTERS

Much of what is positive in life takes place with others. Is there someone you feel comfortable phoning at four in the morning to tell your troubles to? If your answer is yes, you will likely live longer than someone whose answer is no. Isaacowitz, Vaillant, and Seligman (2003) discovered this fact in the Grant study. They found that the capacity to love and be loved was the single strength most clearly associated with subjective well-being at age 80. Invite clients to answer the following questions:

- "Who has supported me or helped me along the way?"
- "What have they done that has been helpful to me?"
- "What positive things would they say about me if I asked them?"
- "How do/did I support the people who support me?"
- "Which other people, who have known me when I was not ill, could remind me of my strengths and my accomplishments and that my life is worth living?"
- "Who would I want to continue to support or help me on my healing path? How can they support or help me?"

Therapists' Well-Being

Pope and Tabachnick (1994) found alarming facts about the work we do: Eleven percent to 61% of about 500 psychologists reported at least one episode of depression during their career, 29% had experienced suicidal feelings, and 4% had actually attempted suicide. In 2006, the American Psychological Association's Board of Professional Affairs' Advisory Committee on Colleague Assistance (ACCA) issued a report on distress and impairment in psychologists. They found that mental health practitioners are exposed to high levels of stress, burnout, substance abuse, and vicarious traumatization. Anyone in the (mental) health community knows about compassion fatigue (see Volume 3: Trauma).

How can therapy be more kind, not only for its clients but also for its therapists? How can therapists prevent becoming anxious or depressed and stay resilient? It is about time to take better care of ourselves by paying attention to what we want to see expand in our clients and in ourselves. Many SF therapists report that they have a lighter workload, more energy to spare at the end of the day, and, ultimately, less stress. Erickson (Rossi, 1980) states that if people emphasize what is positive, on the little movements that take place in a good direction, they are going to amplify these improvements, and this in turn will create more cooperation with other people (partners, children, friends, and colleagues). The same mechanism probably applies in client–therapist relationships.

Clients and therapists usually experience SFBT as a pleasant form of therapy. Research shows that SFBT reduces the risk of *burnout* for those working in mental health care (Medina & Beyebach, 2014).

De Jong and Berg (2002, p. 322) describe the impact of SFBT on its practitioners:

> We spent hour upon hour listening to people's stories about what was wrong with their lives, and felt that in order to be effective, we needed to ask more and more questions about what was wrong. Solution-focused therapy was a breath of fresh air. All of

a sudden, it was the client who determined when they were done with therapy. There were clear behavioral indicators when the goal was reached. We no longer had the burden of being an expert, but worked in collaboration with the client to figure out together what would be helpful. We no longer listened to months or problems, but were listening to strengths, competencies, and abilities. We no longer saw clients as DSM-labels but as incredible beings full of possibilities. Work became fun and felt empowering and our life outside of work was affected as well.

EXERCISE 28. SUCCESS IN WORKING WITH ANXIETY DISORDERS

Interview your colleagues using SF questions about successes:

- "When did you really feel good about your work?"
- "Remember as many details as possible about that time."
- "What factors made sure that you were satisfied?"
- "What exactly did you do that contributed to the success?"
- "What personal qualities did you bring that contributed to the success?"
- "What should you focus on to safeguard (and/or increase) your well-being in working with clients suffering from anxiety disorders?"

EXERCISE 29. CERTIFICATE OF COMPETENCE

Make your own *certificate of competence* (www.johnwheeler.co.uk). The certificate is a self-coaching tool for optimizing professional practice in seven questions.

1. "When I do my work, I take my inspiration from the following people: ———————————"

2. "These people have taught me that when I do my work, it is most important to remember the following: ———————————"

3. "These are the people who encourage me to do the work I do: ———————————"

4. "They encouraged me to do this work because they noticed the following about me: ———————————"

5. "When I do my work, the people I deal with are likely to appreciate that I have the following qualities and abilities: ———————————"

6. "These are the people in my support network who know I have these qualities and abilities: ———————————"

7. "If I am under pressure at work and can only remember one quality or ability, it should be this: ———————————"

To develop a science of human flourishing and achieve the goal of complete mental health, *scientists* should study the etiology of and treatments associated with mental health and develop a science of mental health.

Until recently, the primary emphasis in the *training* of therapists was on pathology. Slowly but surely, there has been a noticeable shift toward a more positive focus. In future training, we have to find a better balance between the focus on pathology and repairing what doesn't work, and the focus on building strengths and resources and what works for our clients and their environment.

Research shows that human strengths such as courage, optimism, interpersonal skills, hope, honesty, perseverance, and flow act as buffers against mental illness. Therefore, therapists should understand and learn how to foster these strengths in people.

The conversational skills in SFBT that invite clients to build solutions are different from those used to diagnose and treat clients' problems. Many SF professionals and trainers believe that adequate therapeutic skills can be achieved with less training time and experience than is the case for other psychotherapies. Research on microanalysis (see Chapter 2) shows that positive talk leads to more positive talk, and negative talk leads to more negative talk. Thus, a therapist's use of positive content contributes to the co-construction of an overall positive session, whereas negative content does the reverse.

It is about time to take better care of ourselves as therapists by adopting a positive stance toward psychotherapy and by paying attention to what we want to see expand in our clients and in ourselves. There should also be a greater emphasis on outcome measurement instead of techniques of a particular therapy model. This change in the research and training of therapists will surely enhance the well-being of both clients and therapists.

SF questions in this chapter are:

96. "What is your partner good at? What do you appreciate in your partner? What aspects of your partner are you proud of? What is positive about your relationship? How did you meet each other? What attracted you in him or her?"

97. "Suppose you woke up tomorrow and your relationship had somehow been transformed to be exactly the way you envisioned it on your wedding day. What would you first notice as evidence of this change?"

98. "What would you like to see different in your relationship? What difference will it make if the other person changes in the direction you want him or her to change? What will be different between the two of you? What will you be doing differently?"

99. "Where on the scale from 10 to 0 would you like to end up (what will be a realistic goal), where 10 equals the best situation possible in your relationship and 0 equals the worst situation possible?"

100. "At what point are you on the scale today (how come it is not lower)? How will you know you are one point higher on the scale? What will be different between the two of you? What will you be doing differently?"

101. "At what point on the scale do you think therapy may end?"

References

Allen, R. E., & Allen, S. D. (1997). *Winnie-the-Pooh on success: In which you, Pooh, and friends learn about the most important subject of all.* New York, NY: Dutton.

American Heritage Medical Dictionary. (2007). (Eds. Houghton Mifflin) Boston, MA: Houghton Mifflin Harcourt.

American Psychiatric Association. (2013). *Diagnostic and statistical manual of mental disorders* (5th ed.). Arlington, VA: American Psychiatric Publishing.

American Psychological Association, Board of Professional Affairs, Advisory Committee on Colleague Assistance. (2006, February). *Report on distress and impairment in psychologists.* Author.I think it was only online, cannot find a location

Arntz, A., & Weertman, A. (1999). Treatment of childhood memories: Theory and practice. *Behaviour Research and Therapy, 37,* 715–740.

Bakker, J. M., Bannink, F. P., & Macdonald, A. (2010). Solution-focused psychiatry. *The Psychiatrist, 34,* 297–300.

Bannink, F. P. (2007). Solution-focused brief therapy. *Journal of Contemporary Psychotherapy*, 37(2), 87–94.

Bannink, F. P. (2008a). Posttraumatic success: Solution-focused brief therapy. *Brief Treatment and Crisis Intervention*, 7, 1–11.

Bannink, F. P. (2008b). Solution-focused mediation. *Conflict Resolution Quarterly*, 25(2), 163–183.

Bannink, F. P. (2009a). *Praxis der Lösungs-fokussierte Mediation*. Stuttgart: Concadora Verlag.

Bannink, F. P. (2009b). *Positive psychologie in de praktijk* [Positive psychology in practice]. Amsterdam: Hogrefe.

Bannink, F. P. (2010a). *1001 solution-focused questions: Handbook for solution-focused interviewing*. New York, NY: Norton.

Bannink, F. P. (2010b). *Handbook of solution-focused conflict management*. Cambridge, MA: Hogrefe.

Bannink, F. P. (2010c). Oplossingsgericht leidinggeven [Solution-focused leadership]. Amsterdam: Pearson.

Bannink, F. P. (2012a). *Practicing positive CBT*. Oxford, UK: Wiley.

Bannink, F. P. (2012b). *Praxis der Positiven Psychologie*. Göttingen: Hogrefe. In the German language capitals are obligatory

Bannink, F. P. (2014a). Positive CBT: From reducing distress to building success. *Journal of Contemporary Psychotherapy*, 44(1), 1–8.

Bannink, F. P. (2014b). *Post traumatic success: Positive psychology and solution-focused strategies to help clients survive and thrive*. New York, NY: Norton.

Bannink, F. P. (2014c). *Handbook of positive supervision*. Cambridge, MA: Hogrefe.

Bannink, F. P., & Jackson, P. Z. (2011). Positive psychology and solution focus: Looking at similarities and differences. *Interaction: The Journal of Solution Focus in Organisations*, *3*(1), 8–20.

Bannink, F. P., & McCarthy, J. (2014). The solution-focused taxi. *Counseling Today, 5*.

Barlow, D. H. (2002). *Anxiety and its disorders: The nature and treatment of anxiety and panic* (2nd ed). New York, NY: Guilford.

Batelaan, N. M., Smit, F., de Graaf, R., van Balkom, A. J. L. M., Vollebergh, W. A. M., & Beekman, A. T. F. (2010). Identifying target groups for the prevention of anxiety disorders in the general population. *Acta Psychiatrica Scandinavica*, *122*(1), 56–65.

Bavelas, J. B., Coates, L., & Johnson, T. (2000). Listeners as co-narrators. *Journal of Personality and Social Psychology*, *79*, 941–952.

Beck, A.T., Emery, G., & Greenberg, R. L. (1985). *Anxiety disorders and phobias: A cognitive perspective*. New York, NY: Basic Books.

Beck, J. S. (2011). *Cognitive behaviour therapy: Basics and beyond* (2nd ed.). New York, NY: Guilford.

Beijebach, M. (2000). *European Brief Therapy Association outcome study: Research definition*. Retrieved May 14, 2002, from http://www.ebta.nu/page2/page30/page30.html

Berg, I. K., & Steiner, T. (2003). *Children's solution work*. New York, NY: Norton.

Brewin, C. R. (2006). Understanding cognitive behaviour therapy: A retrieval competition account. *Behaviour Research and Therapy*, *44*, 765–784.

Brewin, C. R., Wheatley, J., Patel, T., Fearon, P., Hackmann, A., Wells, A., . . . Myers,

S. (2009). Imagery rescripting as a brief stand-alone treatment for depressed patients with intrusive memories. *Behaviour Research and Therapy, 47,* 569–576.

Burns, K., Duncan, D., & Ward, G. C. (2001). *Mark Twain: An illustrated biography.* New York, NY: Knopf.

Cacioppo, J. T., & Gardner, W. L. (1999). The affect system: Architecture and operating characteristics. *Current Directions in Psychological Science, 8,* 133–137.

Carroll, L. (1865). *Alices' adventures in wonderland.* New York, NY: Appleton.

Carver, C. S., & Scheier, M. F. (1998). *On the self-regulation of behavior.* New York, NY: Cambridge University Press.

Cialdini, R. B. (1984). *Persuasion: The psychology of influence.* New York, NY: Collins.

Covey, S. R. (1989). *The seven habits of highly effective people.* New York, NY: Simon & Schuster.

Danner, D. D., Snowdon, D. A., & Friesen, W. V. (2001). Positive emotions in early life and longevity: Findings from the nun study. *Journal of Personality and Social Psychology, 80*(5), 804–813.

Davidson, R. J., Kabat-Zinn, J., Schumacher, J., Rosenkranz, M., Muller, D., Santorelli, S., . . . Sheridan, J. F.. (2003). Alterations in brain and immune function produced by mindfulness meditation. *Psychosomatic Medicine, 65,* 564–570.

De Jong, P., & Berg, I. K. (2002). *Interviewing for solutions.* Belmont, CA: Thomson.

De Shazer, S. (1984). The death of resistance. *Family Process, 23,* 79–93.

De Shazer, S. (1985). *Keys to solution in brief therapy.* New York, NY: Norton.

De Shazer, S. (1988). *Clues: Investigation solutions in brief therapy.* New York, NY: Norton.

De Shazer, S. (1991). *Putting difference to work.* New York, NY: Norton.

De Shazer, S. (1994). *Words were originally magic.* New York, NY: Norton.

Dolan, Y. M. (1991). *Resolving sexual abuse*. New York, NY: Norton.

Duncan, B. L. (2005). *What's right with you: Debunking dysfunction and changing your life*. Deerfield Beach, FL: Health Communications.

Duncan, B. L. (2010). *On becoming a better therapist*. Washington, DC: American Psychological Association.

Duncan, B. L., Hubble, M. A., & Miller, S. D. (1997). *Psychotherapy with "impossible" cases*. New York, NY: Norton.

Duncan, B. L., Miller, S. D., Wampold, B. E., & Hubble, M. A. (2010). *The heart and soul of change* (2nd ed.). American Psychological Association. Washington, DC

Dweck, C. S. (2006). *Mindset: The new psychology of success*. New York, NY: Random House.

Elliot, C. (2012). *Solution building in couples therapy*. New York, NY: Springer.

Epel, E. S., McEwen, B. S., & Ickovics, J. R. (1998). Embodying psychological thriving: Physical thriving in response to stress. *Journal of Social Issues, 54*, 301–322.

Fawcett, J. (2013). Suicide and anxiety in the DSM-5. *Depression and Anxiety, 30*(10), 898–901.

Forsyth, J. P., & Eifert, G. H. (1998). Phobic anxiety and panic: An integrative behavioral account of their origin and treatment. In J. J. Plan & G. H. Eigert (Eds.), *From behavior theory to behavior therapy* (pp. 38–67). Needham, MA: Allyn & Bacon.

Frank, J. D., & Frank, J. B. (1991). *Persuasion and healing* (3rd ed.). Baltimore, MD: Johns Hopkins University Press.

Franklin, C., Trepper, T. S., Gingerich, W. J., & McCollum, E. E. (2012). *Solution-focused brief therapy: A handbook of evidence based practice*. New York, NY: Oxford University Press.

Fredrickson, B. L. (2003). The value of positive emotions. *American Scientist, 91,* 330–335.

Fredrickson, B. L. (2009). *Positivity.* New York, NY: Crown.

George, E. (2010). *What about the past?* BRIEF Forum., www.brief.org.uk

Gilbert, P. (2010). *Compassion focused therapy.* New York, NY: Routledge.

Gingerich, W. J., & Peterson, L. T. (2013). Effectiveness of solution-focused brief therapy: A systematic qualitatative review of controlled outcome studies. *Research on Social Work Practice.* doi: 10.1177/1049731512470859

Gordon, K. C., Baucom, D. H., Epstein, N., Burnett, C. K., & Rankin, L. A. (1999). The interaction between marital standards and communication patterns. *Journal of Marital and Family Therapy, 25,* 211–223.

Gottman, J. M. (1994). *What predicts divorce? The relationship between marital processes and marital outcomes.* New York, NY: Erlbaum.

Grant, A. M., & O'Connor, S. A. (2010). The differential effects of solution-focused and problem-focused coaching questions: A pilot study with implications for practice. *Industrial and Commercial Training, 42*(4), 102–111.

Hackmann, A., Bennett-Levy, J., & Holmes, E. A. (2011). *Oxford guide to imagery in cognitive therapy.* New York, NY: Oxford University Press.

Hayes, S. C., Strosahl, K. D., & Wilson, K. G. (2003). *Acceptance and commitment therapy: An experiental approach to behaviour change.* New York, NY: Guilford.

Hannan, C., Lambert, M. J., Harmon, C., Nielsen, S. L., Smart, D. W., Shimokawa, K., & Sutton, S. W. (2005). A lab test and algorithms for identifying clients at risk for treatment failure. *Journal of Clinical Psychology, 61*(2), 155–163.

Heath, C., & Heath, D. (2010). *Switch: How to change things when change is hard.* London, UK: Random House.

Isaacowitz, D. M., Vaillant, G. E., & Seligman, M. E. P. (2003). Strengths and satisfaction across the adult lifespan. *International Journal of Ageing and Human Development*, 57, 181–201.

Isebaert, L. (2007). Praktijkboek oplossingsgerichte cognitieve therapie [Solution-focused cognitive therapy]. Utrecht: De Tijdstroom.

Isen, A. M. (2005). A role for neuropsychology in understanding the facilitating influence of positive affect on social behaviour and cognitive processes. In C. R. Snyder & S. J. Lopez (2005), *Handbook of positive psychology* (pp. 528–540). New York, NY: Oxford University Press.

Isen, A. M., & Reeve, J. (2005). The influence of positive affect on intrinsic and extrinsic motivation: Facilitating enjoyment of play, responsible work behaviour, and self-control. *Motivation and Emotion*, 29(4), 297–325.

Keyes, C. L. M., & Lopez, S. J. (2005). Toward a science of mental health. In C. R. Snyder & S. J. Lopez (2005), *Handbook of positive psychology*. New York, NY: Oxford University Press.

King, L. A. (2001). The health benefits of writing about life goals. *Personality and Social Psychology Bulletin*, 27, 798–807.

Lamarre, J., & Gregoire, A. (1999). Competence transfer in solution-focused therapy: Harnessing a natural resource. *Journal of Systemic Therapies*, 18(1), 43–57.

Lambert, M. J., & Ogles, B. M. (2004). The efficacy and effectiveness of psychotherapy. In M. L. Lambert (Ed.), *Bergin and Garfield's handbook of psychotherapy and behaviour change* (5th ed., pp. 139–193). New York, NY: Wiley.

Libby, L. K., Eibach, R. P., & Gilovich, R. (2005). Here's looking at me: The effect of memory perspective on assessments of personal change. *Journal of Personality and Social Psychology*, 88(1), 50–62.

Lipchik, E. (1988, Winter). Interviewing with a constructive ear. *Dulwich Centre Newsletter*, pp. 3–7.

Masten, A. S. (2001). Ordinary magic: Resilience processes in development. *American Psychologist, 56*, 227–238.

Medina, A., & Beyebach, M. (2014). The impact of solution-focused training on professionals' beliefs, practices and burnout of child protection workers in Tenerife Island. *Child Care in Practice, 20*(1), 7–26.

Miller, S. D., Duncan, B., & Hubble, M. A. (1997). *Escape from Babel: Toward a unifying language for psychotherapy practice.* New York, NY: Norton.

Miller, W. R., & Rollnick, S. (2002). *Motivational interviewing: Preparing people to change* (2nd ed). New York, NY: Guilford.

Myers, D. G. (2000). The funds, friends and faith of happy people. *American Psychologist, 55*, 56–67.

O'Hanlon, B. (1999). *Evolving possibilities.* Philadelphia, PA: Brunner/Mazel.

O'Hanlon, B. (2000). *Do one thing different.* New York, NY: Harper Collins.

O'Hanlon, B., & Rowan, R. (2003). *Solution oriented therapy for chronic and severe mental illness.* New York, NY: Norton.

Piper, W. E., Ogrodniczuk, J. S., Joyce, A. S., McCallum, M., Rosie, J. S., O'Kelly, J. G., & Steinberg, P. I. (1999). Prediction of dropping out in time-limited, interpretive individual psychotherapy. *Psychotherapy: Theory, Research, Practice, Training, 36*(2), 114–122.

Pope, K. S., & Tabachnick, B. G. (1994). Therapists as patients: A national survey of psychologists' experiences, problems, and beliefs. *Professional Psychology: Research and Practice, 25*, 247–258.

Priebe, S., Omer, S., Giacco, D., & Slade, M. (2014). Resource-oriented therapeutic models in psychiatry: Conceptual review. *British Journal of Psychiatry, 204,* 256–261.

Rosen, S. (1991). *My voice will go with you: The teaching tales of Milton Erickson.* New York, NY: Norton.

Rosenhan, J. (1973). On being sane in insane places. *Science, 179,* 250–258.

Ross, M., & Wilson, A. E. (2002). It feels like yesterday: Self-esteem, valence of personal past experiences, and judgements of subjective distance. *Journal of Personality and Social Psychology, 82,* 792–803.

Rossi, E. L. (Ed.) (1980). *The nature of hypnosis and suggestion by Milton Erickson* (collected papers). New York, NY: Irvington.

Saleebey, D. (Ed.) (2007). *The strengths perspective in social work practice.* Boston, MA: Allyn & Bacon.

Sapyta, J., Riemer, M., & Bickman, L. (2005). Feedback to clinicians: Theory, research and practice. *Journal of Clinical Psychology, 61*(2), 145–153.

Seligman, M. E. P. (2002). *Authentic happiness.* London, UK: Brealey.

Shapiro, F. (2001). *EMDR: Eye movement desensitization of reprocessing: Basic principles, protocols and procedures* (2nd ed.). New York, NY: Guilford.

Siegel, D. J. (1999). *The developing mind.* New York, NY: Guilford.

Tamir, M., Mitchell, C., & Gross, J. J. (2008). Hedonic and instrumental motives in anger regulation. *Psychological Science, 19,* 324–328.

Vasquez, N., & Buehler, R. (2007). Seeing future success: Does imagery perspective influence achievement motivation? *Personality and Social Psychology Bulletin, 33,* 1392–1405.

Walter, J. L., & Peller, J. E. (1992). *Becoming solution-focused in brief therapy.* New York, NY: Brunner/Mazel.

Wampold, B. E. (2001). The great psychotherapy debate: Models, methods and findings. Hillsdale, NJ: Erlbaum.

Watzlawick, P., Weakland, J. H., & Fisch, R. (1974). *Change: Principles of problem formation and problem resolution.* New York, NY: Norton.

Weiner-Davis, M., de Shazer, S., & Gingerich, W. (1987). Using pretreatment change to construct a therapeutic solution: An exploratory study. *Journal of Marital and Family Therapy, 13*, 359–363.

Wells, A. (1995). Metacognition and worry: A cognitive model of generalized anxiety disorder. *Behavioural and Cognitive Psychotherapy, 23*, 301–320.

Wells, A. (1997). *Cognitive therapy of anxiety disorders: A practical manual and conceptual guide.* Chichester, UK: Wiley.

White, M., & Epston, D. (1990). *Narrative means to therapeutic ends.* New York, NY: Norton.

Wittgenstein, L. (1968). *Philosophical investigations* (G. E. M. Anscombe, Trans.; 3rd ed.). New York, NY: Macmillan. (Original work published 1953)

Wood, A. M., Froh, J. J., & Geraghty, A. W. A. (2010). Gratitude and well-being: A review and theoretical integration. *Clinical Psychology Review*, in press.

Ziegler, P., & Hiller, T. (2001). *Recreating partnership.* New York, NY: Norton.

Websites

Association for the Quality Development of Solution-Focused Consulting and
   Training (SFCT): www.asfct.org

Bannink, Fredrike (author of this book): www.fredrikebannink.com

BRIEF, Centre for Solution-Focused Practice, London: www.brief.org.uk

Brief Family Therapy Center, Milwaukee, WI: www.brief-therapy.org

Centre for Solutions Focus at Work: www.sfwork.com

European Brief Therapy Association (EBTA): www.ebta.nu

Gingerich, Wally (with SFBT research): www.gingerich.net

Heart and Soul of Change Project (Barry L. Duncan): www.heartandsoulofchange.com

Institute for Solution-Focused Therapy (Yvonne Dolan) www.solutionfocused.net

Macdonald, Alasdair (with SF research): www.solutionsdoc.co.uk

Miller, Scott D. (with the Outcome Rating Scale and Session Rating Scale): www.scottdmiller.com

O'Hanlon, Bill (author): www.billohanlon.com

Reteaming (Ben Furman): www.reteaming.com

Solution-Focused Brief Therapy Association (SFBTA): www.sfbta.org

Solutions in Organisations Link: www.solworld.org

University of Pennsylvania, Authentic Happiness (Seligman with positive psychology questionnaires): www.authentichappiness.org

Index

Note: Italicized page locators indicate figures; tables are noted with *t*.

About the Author

Fredrike Bannink is a clinical psychologist and a Master of Dispute Resolution based in Amsterdam. She is an internationally recognized keynote presenter and provides training courses all over the world. She is also a Mental Health Trainer for Doctors Without Borders.

Dr. Bannink is the author of 25+ books on SF interviewing, SF mediation/conflict management, SF leadership, positive CBT, positive psychology, positive supervision, and posttraumatic success.

www.fredrikebannink.com